Instant Karma

THE
Heart
AND
Soul
OF A
Ski Bum

Thanks for supporting the Grand Huts Moonlight Ski! Stay on & God Bless

Wayne Sheldrake 03/15/08

WAYNE K. SHELDRAKE

GHOST ROAD PRESS

"Midnight at the Oasis." Notting Dale Songs Inc. (ASCAP) o/b/o itself & Space
Potato Music Ltd. (ASCAP). Used by permission. All rights reserved.

Portions of this work were published previously: "I," in *One Thousand Traces*
by Tim Lovekin and Wayne Sheldrake, 1984; "Love Affair" in *Genesis Literary
Magazine*, 1989; "Watercoler #1" in *Art Times*, June, 1994; "Stare-Out with
the Man-in-the-Moon" *Thunder, Respiration & Meaninglessnesses*, Half Ridge
Press, 1996; a version of "Wave-off" first appeared as "Obituary: Andrew Gray"
in *Mountain Gazette*, January, 2003; a version of "The Face" first appeared
as "The Face, Wolf Creek" in *Mountain Gazette*, December, 2003; a version of
"Another Storm" first appeared as "Into This House We're Born…" in *Mountain
Gazette*, December, 2004; a version of "Outback, Wednesday" first appeared
as "Outback" in *Mountain Gazette*, November, 2005; and a version of "Another
Heart" first appeared as "Opened Heart" in *Your Health Monthly*, February, 2007.

The material in this book is written to the best of the author's recollection.

Library of Congress Cataloging-in-Publication Data.
Instant Karma: The Heart and Soul of a Ski Bum
Ghost Road Press
ISBN (Trade pbk.) 0979625505 ; 9780979625503
Library of Congress Control Number: 2007929023

Ghost Road Press
Denver, Colorado
ghostroadpress.com

Praise for *Instant Karma: The Heart And Soul of a Ski Bum*

"It's not often a writer comes along who can make you laugh and cry at the same time. Wayne Sheldrake is just such a writer. His honest wit, his compassion, and his unerring eye for detail will make you want to follow him wherever he leads. And believe me, he will lead you places you never expected, and for which you will always be grateful."

—Brenda Miller, author of *Season of the Body*, Editor-in-Chief
The Bellingham Review

"With descriptions of blizzards so intense you need a blanket, a hot thermos, and blood pressure gage, Wayne Sheldrake's prose pulls you down his black diamond course of horrific crashes, heart surgeries, and a triumphant race with the of angel of death. Strap on your emergency flares, you're in for one hell of a ride."

—Leslie Lehr, author of *66 Laps* and *Welcome to the Club Mom*

"Sheldrake begins with a bang, into the heart and soul of a bad boy, good-times, adrenaline junkie, careening down mountains and occasionally crashing into trees. This honest and beautifully written book is about a particular, very physical way of being in the world. There's substance to this mad style, philosophy as well as furious fun."

—Sharman Apt Russell, author of *Hunger: An Unnatural History, Songs of the Fluteplayer* and *An Obsession with Butterflies*

"Wayne Sheldrake is a man who goes out of his way to ski in the middle of the kinds of horrible winter storms that keep most of us happily parked in front of the fireplace, beverage in hand. This trait, crazy as it might seem (actually, crazy as it is) leads Sheldrake to epiphanies that bypass even the most enthusiastic skiers. And those epiphanies are worded poetically, even magically, in this book. I'm not even a downhill skier, and I love to read Sheldrake's observations about all things ski-related. There is great stuff within these pages."

—M. John Fayhee, Editor, *Mountain Gazette*, author of *A Colorado Winter*

"Wayne Sheldrake is an estivator. He is the good bad boy. He is a ski bum. He is a thief of skis, ski tickets, down vests, and hearts. He is the Jean Genet of the Slopes. He is the kind of guy who writes poems without punctuation because it's like not wearing underwear, and he scares his parents by faking his own electrocution. He is like a boxer, as proud of his losses as he is of his wins. He has broken almost as many bones as a rodeo clown. And by the way, he is a mighty fine writer whose sentences slalom down the page over every chicanery of rock and clause. There are sentences as scary-fun as the slopes he skis, that glean taste from ratcheted-up emotion, fear from a wild metaphor, and barnacles from the hull of your angst. *Instant Karma* is as much a great book about living as it is a great book about skiing. Your heart, like his, will bang around like a superball in a recipe box."

—Brian Bouldrey, author of *Monster: Adventures in American Machismo*

for Lauren

ACKNOWLEDGMENTS

I would like to thank Matthew Davis and Sonya Unrein for all their help in getting this book published.

Thanks to Ted Conover and Jonathan Franzen for their encouragement.

Many thanks to those who supported me from the beginning: Bill Bradley, John Walton, Tom Miyake, Dean Hubbard, Randy Hubbard, Jodine Ryan, Dr. Robert Buchanan, Dr. Shirley Fredricks, Dr. John McDaniel, Paul Williams, Lynn Weldon, Don Stegman, Dr. Carolyn Harper, Gary Lore and Kathy, Paul and Karen Wagner, Dr. Nason, Kris and Jill Gosar, Greg and Suzanne Gosar, Tracy Gosar, Marta and Steve Quiller, Peter Green, Larry Basky, Barbara Elliott, John and Clara Martinez, Randy Richeson, Craig McDowall, Dennis Kitterman, Tim Hunter, and Bernie Wilkins.

It would take several books to pay tribute to those who inspired me on and off the hill: Rodish, Winberg, Charlie H., Mike, Bill, John, Jeff, Larry, Tom, Tracy, Craig, Todd Wardell, Dru Sanderson, Tim L., Kyle, Phil M., Rick, Reed, Wood, Paul Hall, Jason, Josh, Nad, Aire, Kurt, BDL, Ted, Pat and Page, Phil and Juanita Hall, R. Scott Lamb, and no two more than my mother and my brother Leigh.

Thanks to readers who indulged me: Callie Cochran, Cole Foster, Cynthia L., Geoff and John Weeks, Sam Mills, Bart and Whitney Sheldrake, Agnetti Sheldrake, Aaron Abeyta, Dennis "the Wild Man" McAvoy, Koos Daley, and especially Ted Lay, Phil Davis, and fellow bricklayer David Hayden.

Many at the Creative Writing Program at Antioch University helped with early drafts, including Sharman Russell, Brenda Miller, Leslie Lehr, Brian Bouldrey, and particularly David Ulin.

The following editors have generously given my writing a place in the past few years: Paul Perry, Marilyn Auer, Joe Huckaboo, and John Fayhee of *Mountain Gazette.*

Penultimate thanks to my brother Bart, to Greg and Delen Coin, and to Bob and Sharon Davis—all for their unsolicited generosity.

Finally, my thanks and love to my wife, Lauren (a.k.a. Vreni) and my sons (stepsons), Ryan and Matt. They tolerated years of "typing" and burnt food.

FOREWORD

The first time I moved to the mountains was in 1989. Fresh out of college, as green and dumb as a kid can be, I hightailed it to Aspen. I didn't yet know that Aspen was, well, Aspen. All I knew is that it had the largest bookstore of any ski town in Colorado. Certainly, I wanted to ski, but mostly wanted a place to do research. Back then, mountain towns and local libraries were a contradiction in terms, so that bookstore's coffee shop became my base of operations. I spent whole days in that café, but even the price of a cup of coffee taxed my meager budget. Of course, the rest of Aspen was also too expensive. I ended up living down valley, in the then podunk town of Carbondale, not too far from the spot the late Hunter S. Thompson once called home.

My neighbors were the real deal, mountain folk to the core. Men and women who liked to hunt their own food, drink whiskey, build things, and ski like hell. Wow, could they ski. Every Friday, we would gather at the base of Aspen Highlands for an afternoon game of tag. Highlands was the local mountain, rougher than the others, with all sorts of dangerous nooks and crannies. We divided into two teams: civilians and ski patrol. The game was played at about forty-miles-per-hour. The only time I asked anyone for advice their words of wisdom were short and sweet: "Don't get dead." Don't get dead was good advice, better still since the ski patrol would often handicap our game by taking mushrooms. Hallucinating at high speeds was what passed for fun in these parts—a good lesson in value of life and limb in the mountains, but too much for me. In truth, the whole deal kicked my ass. It took less than a season for my knees to give out, and I gave out with them. It was back to the city for me, to a flatlander's fate, but others stayed—Wayne Sheldrake among them.

It takes a very different kind of person to eke out a ski bum's existence. Most of us, myself included, aren't tough enough to succeed. It's a hardscrabble life of paltry paychecks, broken bodies, and intangible rewards. *Instant Karma* is a story of that life and those rewards. It's a gorgeous tale of high speeds and high stakes, of mountains and the rare transcendence that only mountains can offer. To borrow a phrase from Warren Miller, this is a book about the 'steep and deep.'

Ski bumming may be an alternative lifestyle, but as Wayne likes to point out, "That doesn't mean the lives lived this way aren't real." In fact, as you're about to find out, they're realer than most. Just remember to take a deep breath between pages. The air gets pretty thin in the high hills—you're going to need the oxygen.

—Steven Kotler, Los Angeles, 2007

INTRODUCTION

A couple of seasons ago the marketing department at Squaw Valley provided me with a guide. I'd never skied with a guide before. I didn't need a guide. I figured I'd end up with a ski instructor, get a tour of the trail map, and hear the stock stories—Olympic history, celebrity clients, new village, etc. That didn't happen. I got Larry for a guide.

Larry skied on brown skis, plain brown skis. He liked steep runs near rocks, as steep as staircases and steeper—chutes. We skied all variety of chutes: chutes that zig-zagged between rocks, chutes that swizzled around rocks, chutes that hopscotched rocks, chutes that dived below cliffs. I finally refused above a sliver of snow narrow as dental floss that plunged into a crack no wider than a turnstile.

"No way," I said.

"It's been skied," he nodded.

I knew that meant he had skied it. I asked myself, *Who is this guide?*

By noon my femurs were molten. They felt like they'd bend. I couldn't keep up. Everyone seemed to know Larry. Locals were eager to hop on the quad with us. But they all went the opposite direction at the top. Nobody wanted to ski where Larry was taking me.

I kept thinking, *Who is this guide?*

It got more intense in the afternoon. We clambered over rocks, dirt and weeds—skis on. A patrolman hollered from a cliff above us, "Do you guys need a trail map? There's no access down there." Larry pointed across a face of pummeled granite and dwarf shrubs and hollered back, "This is the access." I grumbled as the edges of my brand new skis sparked on the stones. "You should see my bases," he said. "I don't have any." (Later he showed me the yellow bottoms of his brown skis, stripped like sticks of string cheese.)

Late in the day I followed Larry down a tongue of snow into a chicane of rock walls. I ended up locked in a skidding side-slip down the second of the five "Fingers," a series of short shafts jammed in a monumental fist of granite that punched out from the mountainside. The shaft funneled as it dropped. It shrank to a stone hall exactly 187 centimeters wide. My skis were 186s. The only way out was to leap, let the skis dive and hang on. Extreme skiers call this technique straight-lining. I'm not an extreme skier. I don't straight-line.

As I gained velocity with rocks nearly brushing my shoulders, my thoughts screamed: *Who in God's name is this guide?*

On the chair, one of Larry's buddies congratulated him. Another said, "Yeah. Way to go in Crested Butte." That was a hint. Finally I asked him, "What did you win?" Larry was the 2005 Masters U.S. Extreme Freeskiing Champion. The Championships were held at Crested Butte. Now, at least I knew who my guide was and why there wasn't a chance in hell I'd keep up.

He was mid-forties, my age—still obviously a ski bum, like me. I looked around at the immensity of Squaw. I loved it—gullets and shafts, crowned ridges over deep cleaves, fluted drops into gutters that poured down the abrupt walls of the Olympic Valley. Above it all, snow-filled bowls. Why hadn't I been to this place before? "Why wasn't I here when I was twenty-two?" I asked Larry wistfully.

"If you had been, you'd be a whole different person now."

I knew what he meant. It was a statement of place. He meant the mountain had shaped him—and not just as a skier. As a skier and as a person, a chunk of his being came from the shadows that fell over the banner peaks at closing time and from the jaunty morning sparkle of the opening slopes. Years of leg-wrestling soggy, muscular, Sierra snow molded him. I believed what he meant because I'd only been there a day and already I was a different skier, and a different person, forever. I felt lucky to have a guide.

When I met Larry I was working on this book, with a long way to go. He and Squaw reminded me what three decades of skiing had given me: lots of guides, and guidance. He reminded me of one of my first ski pals, Steve Rodish. For Rodish, skiing was a dare—a big one—to be approached with deadpan composure. Mostly, it was an excuse to get off the ground into the air, longer and farther than anyone around. Speed mattered because faster was better. More speed at the edge of a snowy precipice meant flying longer and farther than anyone around. It wasn't about getting on the snow; it was about getting off the snow.

Steve and Larry even looked similar—short, lean types with octagonal chins. Jeweled eyes scanned faces and landscapes levelly; weathered to-hell-and-back creases webbed their temples. There were other similarities. Like Rodish, Larry had a second love, surfing. Steve's was fishing. Both were carpenters by trade. Neither one ate much, preferring a couple of cups of coffee in the morning. Larry met his wife skiing. Steve, too.

Larry had rules and was quick to loyalty. At one point in the afternoon, I begged him to go on without me. I couldn't stand the idea of slowing him down. "Nope," he said. "You can't quit. It's against the rules: you have to ski until four." He led me into the lift line for one more run at 3:58. Rodish listed his rules by number: RULE #1: Don't get excited. RULE #2: Always get your paycheck. RULE

#3: Try not to look like a hooked trout.[1]

When I was a rookie ski instructor hitchhiking eighty miles one-way to get to the ski area, Steve offered me the couch in his cabin, for the rest of the winter. In return, I was required to help him finish twelve packs of Coors and listen to a tape of Jimmy Buffet ballads over and over again. (...*Yes I am a pirate, two hundred years too late...*)

They both had that knack for the low-key, understated, mighty line—uttered on a mountainside as if it were subtext meant only for you. *If you had been, you'd be a whole different person by now.* Once, also on the side of a mountain, on the last run of the last day of the ski season, Rodish told me, "Everybody's going their separate ways. Some you'll never see again. Some will die before you see them again." He was twenty-three at the time, and the wisest person I knew. I was twenty and he knew that I was naïve enough to believe that everything goes on and on forever. I realize, looking back, that he knew he was already gone.

When Larry invited me for a beer down in the village and insisted on paying (which seemed backwards to me), I realized exactly what was going on. All those chutes—he knew the name of every one of them—they were slivers out of his life. They were what he'd found that it takes a lifetime to find. After a climb up onto a prominent feature, he'd pointed a ski pole down a mind boggling rock crevasse and told me he'd waited seven years to do it—for exactly the right conditions and exactly the right day.

He knew the names of everyone else who had been down that chute, ever. The list was short, and it was a brotherhood. In essence, he was telling me who his guides had been, how the mountain itself

---

1 For the sake of accuracy I have to note that this rule was actually adopted from Charlie Howard, who went on to become one of the "Top 100 Ski Instructors in America." It was Charlie's Rule #1. His Rule #2 was: "A smart monkey doesn't monkey with another monkey's monkey," which Rodish adopted as Rule #4. Rule #5 for all of us was you could only have four rules.

had been his guide. This was how Larry had become who he was.

At the bar he introduced me around to a few friends, including the guy who held the record for the most runs in one day on KT-22, the chair to the formidable—and revered—terrain we'd skied most of the day. The guy was a legend in Larry's eyes. Larry's heroes were friends like that, guys (and gals) who skied on his mountain. The mountain was their common, biggest hero of all. It made them a band. I liked that. That's what Larry and I had in common. We both had our heroes and the biggest among them were mountains.

Two mountains and the friends who skied them have shaped me. Where I ski, in the remote ranges of the Colorado Rockies, has everything to do with what I've become. I met the people I love here. Some of the most important went their separate ways after a season or two. Some died before I had a chance to see them again. Those who stayed became who they are here, with me. It's easy to say we're just ski bums and we just ski, but it's an authentic life. By that I mean it's as valid when it's hard as when it's easy, and it's never as easy as it looks. It's real life.

I saw skiing give my mother relief from an agonizing divorce. I worked my way through college teaching skiing. After college, I taught skiing full-time. I met my wife skiing. Teaching skiing led me to teaching high school. When I taught high school, we skied every weekend and every holiday. I took up ski racing as an adult. My two boys grew up skiing (then, snowboarding). When I had open heart surgery at thirty-three, they watched me get back into shape so I could ski. Because of all that skiing, I didn't go to grad school until I was in my forties. In grad school I started this book. Shortly thereafter, I got a college teaching job. I quit when the winter semester bulletin came out and I was scheduled to teach classes on Friday. My wife supported the decision. We like to ski on Fridays.

For most of my life, I resented summer. I don't surf (sorry Larry) and I've never been much for fishing (sorry Steve), and summer was just a grueling long-ass wait between ski seasons. But recently I figured out how to enjoy summer. I've taken up skiing on sand dunes. I especially like to take friends who have never done it before. They're skeptical. I have to talk them into it.

See, it's a lot of work climbing sand dunes with skis and boots packed on your back. Even I wonder why I'm doing it until I see someone ski on sand for the first time. They smile. They have to. When they push the skis to turn, the sand makes a ripping sound that sounds exactly like a fart. The skis fart all the way down the dune. It's impossible to avoid. It's funny to watch people smile as they fart. And it's fun to do.

Still, I'm fairly certain that none of them would have tried it if I hadn't convinced them to come along. I understand. Like me—for the last thirty years—all they needed was a little guidance.

—Wayne Sheldrake

..and everything is different now.

—Don Henley

ONE

OF A CERTAIN MIND

I remember being appalled as a little boy when my parents left me and my two brothers with a temporary nanny while they took a cruise of the Bahamas. The nanny was a stern woman who wore a starched white dress, tinted nylons, and white shoes. She pinned a wimpled nurse's cap to her netted hair bun. Her name was Mrs. Sailor. She cooked. She cleaned. And she kept constant watch over me. I was likely to sneak off to the cribs of my baby brothers and trounce them as they slept. I might pull down a bookshelf or try to drown a cat. I pestered and taunted her, unplugging the vacuum when she wasn't looking, stomping through piles of sweepings before she could get them in a dust pan.

She had some luck controlling me later in the week when she reminded me that my mother would be coming home soon and that the reports on my behavior would not be good. My sense of foreboding grew as the day approached. After asking how the babies were, my mother asked about me. Mrs. Sailor smiled stridently. "Wayne is a…precocious little boy," she said. I recognized that precocious rhymed with supercalifragilisticexpialidocious, but I didn't know what it meant. I didn't need to. I knew I'd been bad. My mother smiled. "Precocious," she said. "That's a good word for it." As she walked Mrs. Sailor to the door, she may have told the story of how I'd broken my collarbone when I leapt from my own crib. Despite their pleasantries, I knew I was in trouble.

I was more than precocious. I was cruel. I resented that my parents had left me with a stranger while they went somewhere fun and I took it out on the nanny. At some point I became so precocious my parents put a lock on my bedroom door, on the outside—so I couldn't escape and vandalize the house or terrorize my brothers at the crack of dawn, which is exactly what I did when I got the chance. I remember pleading with my mother to leave the door unlocked, in case the Boogie Man showed up. She said the Boogie Man couldn't get in because the door was locked. But what if the Boogie Man was in the closet? I asked. She assured me there was no Boogie Man in the closet. I reminded her that she was the one who told me the Boogie Man might be in the closet. She knew it was a ploy. I didn't believe in the Boogie Man.

At five, I faked my own accidental electrocution. I had my brother run to the other end of the house to get my mother while I lay spread eagle on her bed. I peeked through my eye lashes as she came screaming through the door. A couple of weeks later, I ran away, into the woods. When I saw her car coming down the road, I hid behind a stone wall. I was gone all day and I ended up miles down a country road. I'd left because my father, who was busy with something else, wouldn't play with me. He tried to teach me something when he explained that you have to work before you can play. I didn't like that idea and headed down the road with a plan to make it to the nearest swimming pool. When I got there several hours later, it was empty.

What I remember about being a kid is playing in the woods, alone. We lived on the Pennsylvania countryside. It was like Christopher Robin's woods and I loved it. Then, in first grade, we moved to a Philadelphia suburb. I had to go to school. I got angry and stayed angry. I was telling babysitters to go to hell (and other words) by the time I was six. When I was seven, I threw about forty dirt clods in the neighbor's freshly painted swimming pool. A few days later, I stabbed the boy who put me up to it—with an X-Acto blade, in the eye. It was revenge. He was older and had tricked me. He teased me that I was too little and too weak to throw the dirt clods over my back fence. I didn't know there was a swimming pool on the other side. (Another empty swimming pool!) The same guy had taught me to cuss, because he knew I'd get in trouble for it. I was the kind of kid who hooked his knees around the railing of a Grand Canyon scenic overlook and hung off backwards while his mother went berserk and lost her Ray-Bans in the abyss. That's exactly what I did when we visited the Grand Canyon. On the trip, my much older half-sister—who babysat me long before I became foul-mouthed—finally admitted she'd dropped me on my head once when no one was looking. She still claims it was an accident.

By third grade my parents had moved out West. They divorced. It wasn't friendly, the divorce or the new surroundings. Denver kids made fun of how I talked. They said *wah-ter*, like the word was made with two bricks. I said *whatah*, like it was a fluid you drink. They made fun of my long hair. I could tell they wanted to fight all the time, although I had to ask what they meant when they kept pushing me and saying, *Choose ya*! One day a bunch of kids, boys and girls, followed me after school, egged me and beat me up. I guess no one had ever told them to go to hell in a Philadelphia accent before. When they were done with me, they went on to the next new kid. It was a bonanza for them that lots of new kids were moving in. Eventually I found friends, other new kids, which meant I was never really done with the bullies. They did me one favor. They were the source of my earliest competitive urges. I wanted to beat them, at everything. Sports were my way of fighting back. I wasn't a great athlete, but what I lacked in skill I made up for in intensity that bordered on rage. I practiced and practiced thanks to their mercilessness. At ten, I was diagnosed with a debilitating heart condition and as I grew older the list of sports I was forbidden to play grew longer and longer. Doctors were afraid over-exertion might kill me. They had no idea what they took from me. Now I was angry with doctors, too.

My mother had boyfriends over the years. They were often around for long weekends, away from their wives. A couple of them were okay; they left me alone. Eventually one moved in. He didn't like me. I was only in middle school, but I let him know I didn't like him either. It's almost too sad that he gets credit for the beginning of my ski life, but he was a ski instructor and—I now realize—a true ski bum. He and my mother told everyone at the resort where he worked that they were married. This enabled my mother, my two brothers, and me to ski free, using our "family" season passes. We used our real first names and his last name. I didn't like having his last name attached to mine, but I went along with it, and we all skied both days of every weekend (and many Mondays) for three or four seasons—as poachers. We were all ski bums together.

Mom kicked him out after a few years. Months after I'd forgotten he existed, he showed up in the middle of the night, shouting in our front yard. My mom called the cops before he kicked in the front door. He dragged her down the stairs. About then my brothers and I were waking up. She ordered us to lock ourselves in our bedrooms. She said he had a knife. I had a bat, but I was scared. I wasn't sure what he might do to my mom. He had a knife. I was fourteen at the time, but I felt helplessly younger, and ashamed.

When the cops showed up, I jumped out the window to the roof and off the roof to the ground. They thought I was the perp. Four guns leveled at me from the edge of a spotlight. I ran toward them with my hands up. "I'm not him," I screamed. I followed them into the house and saw my mother in her nightgown. The old boyfriend held her to the floor by the hair. He kept yelling at the cops, "YOU SEE THIS! THIS IS MINE!" He pointed at her with the knife each time he bellowed. I was pushed back out of the house when the cops realized I was there.

Mom had better boyfriends after that. They didn't move in. I liked one guy who always showed up with a six pack and twenty bucks to get my brothers and me to leave the house for a few hours. He wore a black toupee that balanced on his head like a whole rooster wing. I'd developed the habit of staying with friends whenever I could anyway. By high school I was shuttling from one house to another like an exchange student. My mom would have to call around to get me to come home. When my friends and I were old enough to drive, a couple of us ripped off fire extinguishers from the school. We'd drive by keggers attended by jocks and cheerleaders, some of them the same kids who had taunted me and beat me up in grade school, and hose them down with water. One night I added bleach so their clothes would spot. That was the night a guy sprinted two blocks and caught up with us at a clogged intersection. Before I knew he was there, he reached in the car grabbed my long hair and pounded my face while the driver, my friend, mashed on the horn and screamed at the car in front of us to get out of the way. When we finally peeled out to get away, the guy kept a solid grip on my long hair. I still have no idea what he looked like. I guess I'd recognize him if I saw a close-up of his fist.

My senior year, I wrote a poem. Looking back, I see that it was a death poem, although I thought it was a love poem. I thought if I could find a girl who liked it, I might get laid. A lot of it went like this: *If we know love through love we know/If we die with love then life is known/If we know life through death we love.* Dark stuff. Serious stuff. I don't think I was thinking about killing myself, though. I'd quit riding motorcycles when I was fifteen because I was so wild and loved the speed so much and fell off so often I was *sure* I was going to kill myself. I know a lot of people go through a stage where suicide sounds interesting, but in my case I think what got me thinking about death was my bad heart more than despair and confusion, though there was enough of both.

My mother gave me a set of luggage for graduation. I didn't leave until she kicked me out. Who can blame her? I refused to work. Obviously, she didn't want an unemployed eighteen-year-old camped out in the basement writing death poems. I'd have kicked me out, even if the poetry was good. I tried living with my father. He said he would help me with college if I worked for him.[2] It all fell through when I caught him beating his third wife and came to her defense. (I wasn't a scared fourteen-year-old anymore.) Soon after the confrontation he sent a seven page handwritten letter to the University of Missouri/Kansas City Music Conservatory ranting for the rejection of my application. (He didn't realize I'd already been accepted.) He told them I was a lazy bum. He said he would never pay. He warned them that I was, in his words, a "slimy Jew." I know this because he sent me a photocopy of the letter.

Over the next two years I hung around in the city, worked in restaurants, lived in dive apartments. I read Steinbeck, Hesse, Hemingway, Kazantzakis, Kosinski, Vonnegut, Orwell. I carried around a copy of *The Story of Philosophy*, although I never finished it. I underlined long passages in *Lust for Life*. I crossed streets ignoring traffic. I listened to the same Cat Stevens record every night for two years. (*Lord my body has been a good friend/but I won't need it when I reach the end.*) I watched *Harold and Maude* twenty-seven times. I wrote more poetry and continued to not get laid. I didn't

2 My father was a fairly well-known photographer in Colorado in the '80s. He had mastered a complex and artful color photo-processing technique based on large format negatives and sold dramatic landscapes in a gallery he opened in a historic district west of Denver.

drink much, but when I did I got loaded. I became blunt, jesterish, enraged by the pettiest hypocrisies. I didn't like weed, but I tried it a couple of times. All I wanted was to feel far, far away. But by the time someone talked me in to taking a drag I was drunk, and instantly got the spins. Within minutes I was upchucking.

When I found out that my parents' divorce decree instructed my father to pay for the college education of my brothers and me, I initiated a suit. My mother assumed the suit and won. (It helped her, too. He owed her several years unpaid child support.) The sad part was, he had more than enough money, but instead of helping, he wanted to spend it on lawyers. I picked a small school in the sticks of Southern Colorado. It was a beautiful place, farmlands, high deserts, and sand dunes surrounded by mountains that looked like the Tetons. The campus was landscaped with enormous cottonwood trees. I got a weekend job nearby, teaching skiing.

Around then, my parents' story emerged. Their past was pretty twisted. My father's first marriage had been to my mother's older sister. By technicalities, this made my father my ex-Uncle and my Aunt my ex-stepmother. I had a half-brother and half-sister who were also my ex-cousins. Weirder yet, my mom was also my dad's ex-sister-in-law, and his ex-wife was his new sister-in-law. When my father divorced my mother's sister and married my mother, my mother's father was so pissed he never spoke to my mother again, and my mother's mother was forbidden to speak to her, too. In essence, my grandfather and grandmother divorced their own daughter. I forgave my half-sister for dropping me on my head, but I blamed the rest of the dissonance in my life on my father. I earned an academic scholarship in my second year of college and I wrote him I didn't need his money anymore. He was still pretty pissed about getting sued. He was really pissed when I told him to take his check and shove it. We didn't speak again for years. When we finally came to a marginal reconciliation, we mostly talked about baseball.

In my college years, I developed a personal code. I had my own definition of *freedom* and *cool*. My weekends at the ski area became my obsession. Following the lead of a handful of the wildest, most unprofessional ski instructors I could find, I skied as fast as I could. We hucked ourselves off cornices. We built jumps and did flips. We hopped off chairs between lift towers. We had contests to see who could ski the straightest run from the top of the mountain to the bottom. One time, I figure we were going around seventy miles an hour. I did it in duct-taped, wire-framed John Denver glasses. No goggles. No helmet. Coming down a mountain, I felt I was a speed-shaman—indomitable, untouchable. Velocity scrubbed the existential barnacles from the hull of my angst like a belt sander. On the mountain, time itself seemed to be erased. All I needed was a pair of skis. I didn't stop for food. I didn't stop for water. I didn't use sunscreen. (Only pussies wore sunscreen.) I never worried about getting hurt. I didn't think you could kill yourself skiing. It's probably true that sometimes I just didn't care if I died—because I was so happy. Life was so cool then, really cool. I wasn't just a free-spirit. I was free.

I considered danger a kind of addiction, *positive addiction*. It's brain chemistry. It could be worse. It could be heroin. What's so bad about wanting to hold your own destiny in your own hands, even if just for a few seconds? Now when I see kids like that, I just shrug my shoulders, cross my fingers and hope they make it past twenty-three. You can't tell them anything. They've been telling babysitters where to go since they were six. Maybe they'll buy a helmet, quit the potentially fatal stuff, set some boundaries, and settle in for reruns of the *X-Games* before it's too late. Maybe by twenty-five or twenty-six the serotonin thickens a little and they quit dumping perfectly good girlfriends and perfectly good jobs just to go chase their rush. At least, I hope so. Really, nobody wants to end up living with his old drinking buddies when he's twenty-nine.

There was one time I really did want to die. At the end of a long day of skiing I was racing to catch one more ride on the lift before the ski area closed. I miscalculated a turn and hit a tree at about fifty miles an hour. Both bones of my lower right leg snapped like driftwood, completely through. Instantly, I went into shock. It was almost dark by the time the patrol got me off the mountain. In the patrol room, it took about six people to pry my ski boot off. Everyone was freaked by the amount of pain I was in, and they knew getting the stiff plastic boot off my foot without making it worse would be almost impossible. They could also see that I was horrified. I knew the boot had to come off, and I knew my boots were so stiff it hurt when I took them off at the end of a normal ski day. They tried so hard not to hurt me. When the boot did come off, the muscles in my lower leg spasmed, and my whole foot squirmed grotesquely toward my knee. It looked like only skin held it on.

As I was attended to, I realized the people working on me were all my friends. The small room was crammed with people who stayed late after work to help me. This had a profound impact on me. Here were people trying their best *not* to hurt me. I realized I'd felt hurt inside for so long and here were these wild-ass renegades I'd only known for a few months who really cared about me. The ski area was far from the hospital. There wasn't an ambulance. They strapped me on a board and slid me in the back of an old Datsun station wagon. I just laid there and cried. The guy who was driving kept asking me, "Are you okay?" And all I could say was, "I'm okay." I wasn't crying because of the pain. I was crying because I'd never felt so loved.

It was four hours by the time I got morphine. I was already delirious, out of body, nauseous. I drifted in and out of black-outs. I watched a nurse wrestling my limp torso on an examination table. She circled behind me and locked her elbows up under my armpits. A doctor at the other end of the table lassoed my foot with a thick, white rope and then he leaned back and pulled. The skin in the gap between my ankle and my foot stretched like Silly Putty. He was trying to get the foot to stay put at the end of my ankle where it was supposed to be. But when he quit pulling, my right heel slithered back up the front of my shin. My toes and foot rotated inward. It looked like a foot grew out of my shin. Between black-outs, I watched him experiment, leaning this way and that, my foot stretching left and right. The leg muscles stretched as he pulled and then bunched like fists when he let off. The morphine kept pain adrift as long as the splintered bones inside didn't touch, but each yank on my leg brought the raw shunts together. When the broken ends touched, the morphine was like insulation around a thick electrical wire and my body turned to lightning. Finally, to kill the pain completely, I was given a spinal block, which cut off the nerves from the chest down.

Then I was left alone on the table. It's hard to say for how long. I had the motor control of Jello, and I felt like I was falling. I was frantic. I knew I'd slide off the table like a dead fish. Darkness traded with blurred light. I felt myself falling, backwards into a bottomless canyon. There were no rails to hook my knees around this time. There was just the wide gloom of a chasm behind me and a disjointed pair of Ray-Bans plummeting into it. A wall-clock swirled like something out of a Dali nightmare. I watched my good leg, heavy as a ship's anchor, roll off the table. My brain kept trying to lift it, kept sending messages, but the leg wouldn't move. I envisioned being dragged overboard. I saw myself slapping on the tile floor, the broken bones clattering together like nunchucks. The pain of hitting the floor would be as bad as hitting the tree all over again. I was sure my dangling foot would snap completely off if I fell. Delirious, I was convinced I was slipping not just from the table, but toward death. No sleep or drug could save me. The doctor's priestly mutterings echoed in the white corners of the ceiling. I tried to focus on the wall-clock. As it melted away, I saw the second hand, red and slender as a lie-detector stylus, frozen. It was fruitless to fight. Love wasn't enough to make me care. Consciousness was pure pain. It was easier to just let go.

I was in casts for seven months. The casts were designed to make the jagged bone ends rub together. The pain was constant. Even when I kept completely still the leg swelled until it felt like the plaster would explode. Prescription drugs didn't touch the pain. I experimented with my own relieving cocktails. An eight-pack of Little Kings Cream Ale and Pamprin worked best. The mix was almost as bad as the morphine. I dreamed the accident over and over again, jolting awake at the moment of impact. A burled lump of bone eventually formed, rejoining the splintered ends of my tibia and fibula. It bothered me that the leg didn't heal straight, but I cheered up when I finally got to ski again, which was a couple of months before I was able to walk without a limp. My bent leg added to my status among the guys I hung out with. They knew that most people who ski into trees die, and they treated me like a resurrection. My first week back on the mountain, I nearly refractured the green bones in a crash off a big jump.

I was a little confused when I passed my twenty-fifth birthday. I'd never thought I'd live beyond twenty-four. I assumed my stunts would catch up with me, or my heart would just quit. But I was happy because I knew how I wanted to live and if I died in the process, so be it. *If we know life through death we love*, or something like that. I was awarded my bachelor's degree and then made a half-assed attempt at a master's degree, but all I wanted to do was ski. I dropped out, rented a little house down by the railroad tracks. No phone. No TV. I continued to collect fractures and stitches, my red badges of courage. In the summer I kept my stuff and myself in an abandoned trailer with no water, electricity or heat. I used stolen milk crates for furniture. I had my code to live by. I was vegetarian. I hitchhiked. I sought out desolate, spectral quiet. I was attracted to tragic, displaced people and listened to the stories of how they had become lonely. They were my family. I did buy a car when I was twenty-five, a '72 Oldsmobile Delta 88 Royale with a power convertible roof. It cost me a day's wages to fill the tank and I never had insurance, so I didn't drive much. But when circumstances turned sour, I'd drive a hundred miles an hour out on a vacant grid of farm roads. I'd turn the headlights off and drive by moonlight.

I've had a lot of friends who did crazy things—sky divers, extreme skiers, bigwater kayakers, rock climbers, hang gliders, solo trekkers, outfitters, cowboys—guys who did risky things all the time. Every one of them had a story or two about how dumb he was and how he almost screwed up and died, and what a rush it was. They shook their heads and talked about how lucky they were. The honest ones admitted they got off on it—on knowing they'd almost died. One guy I knew almost starved to death when he tried to survive a winter in the wilderness. He wanted to escape the entanglements of civilization. He remembered a long, cold night in which he was sure a spirit was relighting a candle that he kept snuffing. He'd wake up and the candle was lit again. He still has bad teeth from the scurvy. Camping until you're starving isn't really my thing, but I can see what he had in mind.

To almost die and then live—it's wild. Surviving terror can lead to a kind of joy that makes the traumas of "real life" seem less intimidating. Common emotional stresses become blasé. Your weird family life and your personal problems don't really seem that deep. Not that you're suicidal. It just means some people have to get close to death to really figure life out—really close, so when they back off whatever it is they thought was so bad, it doesn't look so bad anymore. If you're lucky—if you have a normal brain—you probably have the advantage of this perspective without a real life near-fatal experience. It might be enough to *feel* like you could have died and then *feel* relieved you're alive. A lot of amusement park rides provide this feeling. I guess that's why we have amusement parks, and why so many people go—to get that *feeling* out of their system. Otherwise everyone would be as crazy as I was, trying to figure things out.

Either that, or they'd be dead.

TWO

INSTANT KARMA: CONFESSIONS
OF A SKI BUM, PART I

I went to college to get out of the city, to get away from my parents, and to avoid work. I started as a vocal music major. I'd been in the Colorado All-State Choir my senior year of high school, and thought I was going to become a high school choir director. I met a nice girl almost right away, an alto, and although I kept a dorm room, I moved into the little bungalow she shared with a second-soprano and a bass player. She and I split her portion of the rent. Our room was a tiny enclosed back porch, so I kept most of my things, including my skis, in the dorm. It's possible she didn't know I skied. Around Thanksgiving, flyers appeared on campus bulletin boards:

FREE SKIING!
SKI INSTRUCTORS WANTED
NO EXPERIENCE NECESSARY
CONTACT WOLF CREEK SKI SCHOOL

Wolf Creek was one of the smaller ski areas in Colorado. An hour-and-half drive from campus, it perched on the top of the state's southern-most range. I'd never skied there.

Until I read that flyer, I didn't know I wanted to be a ski bum. The instant I read it, I knew. I went back to my dorm room and typed a two page letter to the Wolf Creek Ski School begging them to hire me. I called and got the dates for the "hiring clinic," and on the first Saturday of December I awakened in the dark of a subzero morning, loaded gear in a pack, shouldered my skis,[3] and hitch-hiked seventy miles to Wolf Creek Pass.

The Wolf Creek Ski School director was a tall, broom-mus-tached, green-coated, squeaky-voiced hybrid—part aerobics instructor, part revival preacher. He'd been a supervisor for the Aspen Ski School. He announced to me and twenty other candi-dates that we would be competing for seven jobs. He insisted that we "Look up!" and "Smile!" as we gathered in circles to wiggle absurdly short skis on flat snow. He taught us absurdly embarrass-ing on-snow calisthenics. They were the foundation of a technique that was supposed to transform the sport by teaching beginners how to parallel, skipping the clunky snow-plow stage. Supposedly, if you learned on short, short skis, you could be an intermediate skier in a matter of hours rather than weeks or months.

This wasn't at all how I'd learned to ski, so at night I studied mimeographed handouts that described the sequences, sets, and reps of the exercises. I took my turns leading my fellow wan-nabes—unemployed locals dressed in checked flannel shirts, boot cut jeans, work gloves, and parkas that looked like sleeping bags. We hopped. We wiggled. We shuffled. We sweated. We thrashed around like junior high kids mocking our parents' enthusiasm for Chubby Checker's "Let's Twist Again." The ski school director cheered from the sidelines, clapping his thick mittens and barking, "Isn't this fun!"

I kept smiling. *Free skiing*, I told myself. *Free skiing*.

My interview tactics were unpolished. When it came time to have my skiing ability evaluated, I inadvertently bitched out the assistant ski school director for standing exactly where I was trying

3 A pair of Head XR1s, a foam core cracked-edge design, mounted with Salomon 555s, complete with safety straps. The guy who almost knifed my mother had left them behind.

to ski. It didn't hit me that I had just yelled at my potential future boss. He was just some guy standing in my way. I got lucky and linked a few turns through some atrocious shin-deep wind-crust as he watched me go by. Then I waited at the bottom of the slope. He skied directly to me.

He was a sprite, freckle-faced guy in his early thirties. Vermillion hair stalked down from the band of his green beanie. I admired the athleticism of his style. He had the agility of a pine martin, and he completed turns with confident flourish. His skill was obvious, enhanced by his impressively long boards, twice his height, slicing with ease through the cluttered snow. His tracks crossed mine to form a chain of figure eights. I prepared for a reprimand.

"How old are you?" he asked.

"Twenty," I said, backing up a little.

"Twenty," he said. He turned his tails and looked back up the broad slope, a glove shading the sun from his glacier glasses. The steep mountain face was draped with afternoon shadows and littered with fallen and struggling instructor-candidates. "I guess I was in your fall line," he said, still looking back up the hill.

Shit, I thought. *No free skiing for me.*

"Twenty's way too young to be skiing that junk that well," he said. He turned to me. A smile, like notebook paper turned sideways, pushed his cheeks up under the mirrors of his glasses. "I guess I'll have to hire you." He paused. "You'll have to shave your beard, though."

I probed the snow with my ski poles. My first beard. It wasn't much, just blond scruff, sort of like a handful of haircut swept up off the barber's floor and stuck to my face, but it had taken a semester's effort. "Damn," I said.

"I know," he said. "I had to shave mine, too."

By Christmas break, a couple of veteran instructors offered me couch space in a matchbox cabin at the base of the pass. I called my girlfriend. "You're not coming home?" she said, in a voice that sounded even lower on the payphone.

"I'm going to stay up here," I said.

"So when are you coming home?" she said.

"I don't know," I said.

There was a long alto silence. I hung up. I didn't drop out of school—yet—but for the rest of that season, I spent every spare moment on the mountain.

I was hired to teach at $26 a day, plus a dollar a head—*if* I worked. Pay was strictly commission. In a lesson with ten students, that worked out to $36 a day. Pretty good pay for a college student, and theoretically, I still had three free hours to ski. Theoretically, I didn't ski at all for the first two weeks. The Rockies were in the throes of an early winter drought. When word got out that Wolf Creek had sixty inches of snow, dozens of charter buses from all over the state packed the parking lot. They had plates from the South and Midwest. Originally they were bound for Breckenridge or Winter Park, but they diverted their trips when they found out Northern Colorado didn't have any snow. Folding doors opened, and hundreds of beginners poured out. In my first ten days as a ski instructor, I taught four hour-and-a-half lessons a day. Twenty students crammed into each lesson. I didn't stop to eat. I didn't stop for water.

Teaching skiing was surprisingly hard. It was unseasonably hot that Christmas and for days on end I side-stepped, skated to catch loose skis, climbed to adjust someone's malfunctioning equipment, skied backwards to brace students struggling with balance and control. The clientele were lowlanders—ribs, red-beans, and corn-bread folk. Many were stunned, frazzled, dizzied, and dehydrated by the high altitude. When they fell, they slithered in the snow, like catfish in mud. The athletic ones fell even more often, fuming mad because their waterskiing and team roping skills meant nothing on snow. Tired and hungry, I still signed up for the last lift ride of the day, to make an extra $4 helping the Ski Patrol move straggling skiers off the mountain at closing time.

Back at the cabin, I helped my new friends drink down twelve-packs of Schlitz and Old Milwaukee. They fed me elk they'd poached. We played the same Jimmy Buffet tape over and over, and I soaked up their stories about the advanced classes they'd led to the top of the mountain. I made $1000 in less than two weeks. I promptly cashed my first paycheck at what was then the closest "bank," the liquor store at the bottom of the pass.

The San Juans were still "Down Under" back then. Wolf Creek had one center-poled double-chair, a couple of second-hand surface Pomas, and a mile of boundary along a sharp ridge. The day lodge was a timber beam A-frame with a home-sized kitchen behind a counter at one end. At the other, a nook under a staircase served as a bar. The stairs led to the ski school "locker room," an uninsulated attic with coat hooks down the center and hinged-top benches along the sides. A nautical sized bathroom, a rental shop, a snug ski patrol room, and a ticket office were crammed into a walkout basement.

I was a bad example as a professional ski instructor. I was insubordinate and frequently scolded—for attempting flips (a liability no-no), for jumping cornices during classes, for skipping meetings and shifts, for scalping tickets in the parking lot. Besides being a general pain in the sidecut, I skied recklessly, breaking my wire-rimmed glasses in fall after fall. I repaired them with duct tape.

I wasn't the only renegade. By March, half the full-time instructors on a staff of less than fifteen had been fired or quit. Either they'd rejected the silly swivel-hip, short ski technique of teaching, or they weren't smiling enough. Amidst the mutiny, I moved up the seniority list, and I taught full-day lessons every day I showed up.

I ended my first year of college with money in the bank and eager to ski full-time.

Over the next ten years, I started seven seasons at Wolf Creek. I was fired twice, quit twice, and finished two seasons collecting Workman's Comp. In 1982, I did drop out of school to teach full-time. It wasn't always the greatest job. I made $127 that February. There was dead-work. Instructors were expected to mingle with the public and hustle up customers from the ticket line in the morning, but there was no guarantee you'd be assigned to the clients you signed up. Once stiffed, you were required to stay "at work," on the outside chance you might be needed for an afternoon class. To free ski in the meantime, you had to remove your uniform, put on your own coat and pick up a lift ticket at the window. That way, if you got hurt, the ski area could assert that you were not on the clock and avoid paying Workman's Comp.

Thanksgiving, you prayed for good snow. Christmas, you worked everyday for two weeks straight, including all day Christmas Day. Spring break meant no days off for the entire month of March. You piggy-backed as many classes as you could, regardless of the weather or fatigue. It's a harvest mentality: make the money while the money's around. Between the holiday rushes there was plenty of time for free skiing. One December day, I was out teaching lessons for seven straight hours with the temperature hovering around -10. When I finally sat down and cracked the seal on my ski boots that evening, the tips of my toes were black and brittle as hard candy. I wasn't alarmed. It had happened before. I made good money that day, and I was back in my boots the next morning drumming up business like a circus-barker.

I loved it.

THREE

THE FACE

I always thought the massive winter storms that slammed Wolf Creek Pass collected in Canada and funneled down the Rockies. Then a ski patrolman told me, no, the really big systems "get knocked-up" somewhere over Manchuria. He said, they "gestate" as they arc over the Aleutians and by the time they hit the San Juans they're "full-term and head first." I was just a ski instructor and we were six days into a storm that ended up lasting ten, so I believed him.

In those ten days, the light never got brighter than a garden-level apartment. The unending matrix of falling snow had me hallucinating. I was broke, too. Business was slow. A ten day blizzard isn't the best time to take a ski lesson. Front after front—in the end seven bulging systems, each stretching from the Bugaboos to Baja—rear-ended each other and piled on our range like a train wreck. To kill time, I skied what seemed like one endless powder run.

The storm broke into intermittent flurries for a couple of days, then, the last few days of January, a *grand mal* heaved eighty-eight inches of snow in thirty-six hours. The pass was shut down for four days. My 1980 Subaru, which had seized in the ski area parking lot, was buried like a peanut in a quart of Rocky Road. Even twenty miles east of the pass, horses were buried up to their bellies. Early February was sunny, but by mid-month more storms over China fed on a streaming Arctic rotation that threw off long boomeranging columns of humid, cold air. Through the first week of March, fronts came charging, rolling over the Rockies like tank columns over barbed wire. Ten inches. Six inches. Thirteen inches. With ski crowds at home waiting for the roads to clear, the entire ski area staff couldn't track it up.

In one night, a whumph of twenty-eight inches dropped. Gale swept, another eighteen frothed in by noon. Flags outside the lodge thrashed like salmon tails in a spillway. Under a table in the balcony of the lodge, I was napping off a long night of tequila shots. I used a half-gnawed roast beef sandwich for a pillow.[4] I watched the storm through the vertical slit of one eye. The snow seemed to explode into existence, a white fire driven by its own cold fusion. Ground blizzards blasted up. Fat, lopsided twisters unzipped themselves and drilled into flopping spruce. The storm had the crush of surf, slamming incessantly. The wind kept kicking the front doors open until someone locked them. On the deck, picnic tables disappeared under deep, white mounds.

A couple of my fellow instructors slogged in off the flats, moustaches sagging like dish rags. Their green coats came off sweaty and dropped like saddles on chair backs.

"What'd you do?" I mumbled. "Snowshoe through a carwash?"

"Unskiable," they said. "You can't turn in it. Too deep. Even on The Face. We had to dig out every turn. It took forty-five minutes to break trail."

Out the great windows, I saw a big Thiekol snow-cat cross under the upper chairlift and churn directly into the storm, packing behind it a smooth driveway, two king-sized mattresses wide.

4 The drink of choice was a Wyoming. What's a Wyoming? You snort a line of salt; head butt the lime; take a shot of José; then get your Hulk hands on and growl, "WYOMING! DRINK IT!" Keep some Kleenex handy.

One empty chair after another circled the bow-wheel, rose silently, and disappeared into the blur. *Can't turn?* I thought. *Too deep?* In the time it took me to boot up and button down, not one skier had appeared from the upper mountain. I still had the sting of citrus in one eye and my blood sugar was in the basement, but *somebody* had to ski it. Suddenly I wasn't depressed or bored. I was angry, mostly because out of pure ornery *machismo* I had to go prove this storm could be skied.

I backed out a side door like a diver dropping into the wake of a speeding boat. Five minutes up the lift, my toes were hard as walnuts. It was too cold to be wet, too wet to be cold—and ruthlessly both. The snow came like dump trucks of Slurpies chucked into a merry-go-round of jet turbines. My coat took on water like a sponge. I could only hope that the material would act as a wet suit and the water soaking through would warm a little as it coated my skin. The chairlift climbed the steep right flank of The Face. There wasn't a ski track on it.

At the crest—11,700 feet—I was moments from true suffering. The walk around the unloading ramp was like snowshoeing through a carwash. Blasts of wind pushed me left and right, my ski edges scrawling for purchase. I used the edges like ice-climbing crampons to bite into the crust. I waddled to the overlook of The Face. The closer I got to it, the deeper the snow.

Far down in the whiteness, I heard the diesel growl of the Thiekol. There was nothing but bottomless, heavy snow between me and the road it was packing. I knew I'd be all right if I could get down there. On the smooth track, I'd be able to get back to the lodge easily. I thought about what my buddies had said, about the long hike out. They were better dressed than I was. Probably they had better circulation. My feet had been damaged by years of repeated frostbite. Maybe they were smart enough to quit before the storm got colder and wetter. If it took me forty-five minutes to get back, I'd be in trouble. What if I fell? Lost a ski? Got stuck upside down? The skiing was no sure thing. I'd been in snow in this very spot that was so deep and so heavy it was devoid of response. The skis dive under and a flaccid mass collapses on top of them. I'd seen people on The Face sucked down until snow stacked up chest-high, like white mud. Straight back down the lift line would be the best route. It was steep, maybe 40° for the first two hundred feet. I'd need all the momentum I could get to clear a knoll about half way down. If I bogged down there, I'd be digging. What if the snow fractured and slid? Who would know I was there? The chairs that levitated and slid by above me were empty. If an avalanche trapped me, I might not be dead by the time anyone noticed, but the frostbite would be serious and spreading. Frostbite turns your skin as black as a black eye. The skin blisters and bloats. Tissue dies. Stay frozen for too long and there's only one treatment: amputation. One of my toes was already frozen solid.

I aimed for that steep flank under the chairlift. The skis—208 centimeter racing skis—picked up speed, but they didn't float. They sank. I was in snow to my knees. Then the skis dove and I dropped in up to my neck. I felt like an undertow was taking me down. The only way to resist the suction was to dive face-first into the whiteness. I held my breath. Snow splashed on my goggles and poured down the back of my parka. I felt like I had stepped off a high dive and now, under the surface, my feet dangled weight-lessly into cold depths. I was sure the whole hillside had broken away and taken me with it. *Avalanche.* But almost as I determined my oblivion, I felt lift, suspension. I felt the snow holding me as it moved. The drifting sensation was vaguely aerodynamic. I fought to stay upright, my arms swimming forward. I dropped the handles on my poles and grabbed at the snow. I stretched my legs, reach-ing for the bottom, for anything stable. If I squirmed hard enough, the flow seemed to match the yaw and pitch of my descent. Snow wrapped around my chest, wrapped my thighs as I surged along. My head went under.

Miraculously, my bindings had not released. I prayed my skis would stay with me. Without one, I'd be handicapped. If I lost both, it would be a lonely, cold walk off the mountain. Though I was gaining speed, I pointed the skis straight. I feared the slightest wag of either one would tug me deeper and pull one off. Panicked and submerged, I gasped for air. I gulped a fist of snow. It was like sucking cold exhaust. Now I wanted to go even faster, because I was choking and I wasn't sure I could hold my breath long enough to make it to the bottom. I'd heard of skiers in Utah using snorkels. I'd heard of skiers drowning upside down in collapsed tree wells. Was it possible to drown right side up? It was quiet. I was oddly aware of the snow's hiss as it moved up the front of my coat and cascaded over my shoulders. Swarms of feathery snow mashed against the lens of my goggles and peeled away from the plastic. Visibility: one inch.

The skis came alive with their own pendulous consciousness. This happens sometimes. You feel like the skis know more than you do, as if they're possessed of their own tactile sentience, infused with their own sixth sense. You let them go and follow. I felt them veer enough to mimic the incline of the slope. I stretched to get my neck above the surface. I was suffocating. Although moving seemed imperative and the snow moved faster and faster, the speed frightened me. First of all, I was blinded by pure whiteness. Second of all, I don't usually ski straight down steep runs. It had to be an avalanche.

I had skied The Face hundreds of times in all sorts of conditions. I realized how heavily I depended on my vision. One of the comforts when skiing steep slopes is seeing the bottom. Even if it's far below, it's a tangible goal. Think of the baby making his first long, uncertain walk across a living room of shag carpet. If his eyes lock on his mother across the room, the fear is tamable. In the dark, that same walk is impossible, awash with terror. No bottom in sight, I was alone with my fear. Rationally, I knew The Face dropped at a sharp angle for two or three hundred feet, then gradually flattened, the entire run comprising about a quarter of a mile of terrain. I also knew that if I was descending anywhere close to the route I had chosen from the top, somewhere out there was a lift tower. If the snow that carried me spilled into it, so would I. It was like falling into a dark elevator shaft and wondering what floor the elevator was on. The snow maintained its speed. I found equilibrium in it, somewhat like a sky-diver guiding himself in a defined channel of air. It sloshed urgently, like water through a down spout. It plunged, pushed me, and I plunged with it.

But then, it suddenly slowed; it stalled. For a moment it felt thicker and deeper. It swirled, as if I'd dropped into a tight, soupy eddy. I swam to keep from being twisted around. Inexplicably, lower layers released as the rest of the snow gained momentum again, taking me with it. The snow stalled and started, stalled and started, which scared me as much as the falling. I felt if I stopped, I would be hopelessly stuck, buried, my whereabouts unknown. With each pause, I paddled forward frantically, hoping the turbulence would eventually release down the hill again. The snow plunged again, like a bomb-bay door falling open, taking me with it. Amidst the panic, I had one flashing comfort. The pulsation of the movement—like a slow heart—convinced me that, at least, I was not in an avalanche.

I understood why my buddies called the snow unskiable. I could extrapolate what had happened. When they tried to turn, their skis were immediately sucked under, like floating Popsicle sticks spinning toward a drain. The snow came too deep and too fast. It couldn't hold its own weight. It was a house of cards. It simply collapsed when a skier moved through it. Normally, a powder skier expects skis to scoop into the snow and then scallop toward the surface. As the skis rise up, they feel light and easy to turn. That's what powder skiing is all about, the ethereal, fluid sensation of floating from curl to curl. But in these conditions, the snow collapsed faster than a turning ski could move. My pals were buried to their hips because they tried to turn. But the only way to make it through was to move faster than the snow collapsed. I had no choice but to go as straight as possible and ride the current.

I felt the slope get flatter. My goggles and then my whole head emerged from the surface like a periscope. A moment later, I popped through a wall the snowcat had carved out. The emergence was a shock. Suddenly I needed to balance on my feet. I felt gangly and weak, like I was stuffed with straw. The skis squirted across the packed snow, dragging me along. I threw them sideways, frantically chopping the edges into the cushy track. I leaned over my ski poles. My lungs raled for air, as if I had just swum the length of a swimming pool underwater. I choked. My eyes watered. I looked back up the hill. I saw the luminous blizzard, shadowy lift towers, and empty chairs passing each other in the white smear. The fury of the wind filled my ears straight through my hat. It seemed like an hour ago I had been on top of the mountain looking down and hoping.

Instantly, I knew I was going back up.

It had been quiet and oddly warm when I was enveloped. I was seduced by the fibrous, cloying flotation. My extremities, even my numb feet, suddenly felt flush. I liked the risk of being alone. I liked that I'd skied what they called unskiable. I liked it that I felt a million miles from anywhere. I liked it that no one else would ever know exactly how I did it, and probably wouldn't believe me anyway. I liked that I could hardly believe it myself. I wanted to do it again and again. I wanted to remember this—forever. I had to go back up. Still gasping, I tucked and followed the high sidewalls of the cat track. I forgot about the frostbite and the lift tower. I forgot that every new inch of snow increased the risk of avalanche. I convinced myself that the only way to stay warm and survive was to keep skiing.

On the chair ride, I scanned the shrouded mountain for my tracks. There were none—at least nothing that looked like ski turns. The snow I'd flumed through was tossed, like the berm of a *Caddyshack* gopher tunnel. The furrow descended as a random drip might run down a page of tilted watercolor paper. My "tracks" were nothing but an opaque scar. My submerged body had hoed through and the brief wake had collapsed on itself, behind.

I went back up five, six times, more. I skied in exactly the same place reliving exactly the same sensations, except I got better at holding my breath. At the edge of each run, before I dove under again, I purposely hyperventilated, gulping at the abrasive wind. At the top, the storm was dropping an inch of snow every fifteen minutes. The wind blew fifty miles an hour. *One more time*, I kept telling myself. For ten runs, I laid out face-first across the silky parachute-whiteness and watched snow peel like ant farm sand across the lenses of my goggles.

I was doing something I'd never done before and never dreamed of doing, and that hadn't been done before—at least not on that run, not on that day, not in that storm. Even when I knew my metabolism had dropped dangerously—my breathing short, my heart slow, my body temperature dipping—I kept going up. On the chair, I clasped my wet coat and locked my knees together, shivering. My elbows creaked like rusty hinges. My hamstrings contracted to tight bands. My stomach hollowed and shrank. My shoulders slouched and hardened against the maw. I remembered thinking that a storm like this and snow like this might never come again; and now I think if it ever does, it will take as long as an old half-forgotten comet, coming to indicate the end and death, when all I'll be able to do with my thin will and thinner bones is watch it pass in the distance.

Finally, the storm got wilder, warmer and wetter. The snow succumbed to itself, settling in tough, stratified layers. The wind pounded a top-crust. The cat-track drifted in. The flat light went convex. I slogged into the lodge, threw down my drenched, green coat, sat in a chair and shivered. My pals had been sipping cocoa and watching me do laps.

"How was it?" they asked, with sadistic satisfaction.

"You were right," I said. "You can't turn in that stuff."

They grinned, their mustaches, brushed and dry now, tipped with whipped cream.

I finished my roast beef sandwich, dried out a little, and crawled back under my table in the balcony. If I slept, I didn't sleep deeply, because I remember watching through the vertical slit of one eye as the storm went on and on. Empty chairs descended from the wooly crawl of the blizzard, about-faced on the bow-wheel and climbed back into the squall.

FOUR

INSTANT KARMA: CONFESSIONS
OF A SKI BUM, PART II

Vreni was a dream of the stretch pants era. Her legs were firm from ballet classes and lap swims. We met in the Wolf Creek Lodge. I was a veteran instructor, admiring the new girl as she bent to buckle her ski boots. Abruptly, she turned. "Hi," I said. "I'm Wayne, and…" She'd caught me gawking. She had long brunette hair and eyes the color of an autumn meadow. Our first "moment"—aside from me gawking at her tight ski pants—came when she literally fell off the Continental Divide. The entire Ski School had been assigned to pre-season boot-packing—a method of avalanche control which involves stomping deep holes into slide prone snow. On the hike out to the area boundary, Vreni lost her balance, fell off the edge of the ridge, and slid away at high speed on her back head-first into the shadows of a steep bowl. I snapped into my skis and chased her. At the bottom, I realized she was laughing, hysterically. I liked that.

Recently divorced, she'd moved from Ft. Worth to Colorado. I asked her if her ex was mentally ill. "What?" she asked. I said, "Anyone who would leave you has to be mentally ill." Our first kiss was near the end of a ride on a double chair. Our first date, a dinner of Oreos and red wine, was fireside in a remote mountain cabin. A few nights later, I bribed a barroom full of drunks with a round of Jack Daniels, gathered them in front of the pay phone next to the pool table, and we sang her "Happy Birthday." She invited me up to her cabin, far up a frigid mountain valley. Her two little boys were excited to meet me. We played with some toy cars for awhile, and the three year old asked me, "Are you going to spend the night?" I looked at Vreni, smirking. Then the oldest said, "We have a phone. You can call your wife and ask her if it's okay." Vreni and I burst out laughing. The oldest found me asleep on the couch the next morning. "So," he said, "I see you did spend the night."

Not long after Vreni and I met, I almost died, again. I was skiing fast. A skier blindsided me, knocking me into the trees. At the time, everyone blamed the kid who hit me. I tried hard to come to the same conclusion, but the more I thought about it the more obvious it became that I could have prevented the confluence of events that led to the accident. I'd been leading an expert class to the bottom of the mountain when a student behind me lost control and accelerated to a reckless speed. He crashed into me at the bottle-neck of a narrow trail. I was thrown into the trunk of a large spruce. I never felt the impact. I blacked out. I awoke sprawled in the snow, wrapped backwards around the tree. Though I was out for just a few seconds, it felt like I'd been out a long time, like I'd been asleep. When my eyes opened, the sun was brighter than I'd ever seen it, but my body was frozen. I was paralyzed. *So, this is it,* I thought. *This is how life will be. Paralyzed.* I was surprised that I felt peaceful and warm. I lay in the snow looking up at a steep slope, a shining glade of scattered pines—a great ski spot.

My head was turned to the side, cradled in the soft cusp of the tree drift. From there, I realized I could see the spot where my leg had snapped like a wish-bone. The first tree had been cut down for a new trail. Now, here I was less than twenty-five feet from where I'd laid in shock with compound fractures of the tibia and fibula five years before. My view from the ground was almost exactly the same. I was stunned as much by this unbelievable coincidence as I was by the percussion my body had just absorbed. I remember thinking it would be a long life: paralyzed. I was still young.

A woman nearby stepped out of her skis, knelt beside me, and shoved her bare hands between the snow and my head. I recognized her. She knew me. She'd helped manage the ski area the very first year I was hired. I hadn't seen her in years. She shivered and cried uncontrollably, apologizing when her tears dripped in my face. All I could do was try to control my lungs. They heaved involuntarily, violently. A crowd gathered. They looked down at me as if I were a spectacularly deformed trout gasping in a bed of grass.

I tried to move my fingers and toes. At first nothing, but then the ends wiggled. As the paralysis melted away, I went from icy immobility to a nightmare of ferocious pain. My right thigh and my lower back felt like they'd been attacked with a sledge hammer. I struggled to stay conscious. I remembered all this; five years ago felt like yesterday. I remembered the shock and I knew all I could do to help myself was try to get control of my breathing. It took bizarre, meditative focus, but I knew if I didn't calm my spasming lungs, I'd black out. Then I'd be at the mercy of the shock.

By the time a ski patrolman arrived on the scene, I'd been able to reach behind me and inspect my spine. It seemed straight. I told him I'd broken my femur. I'd heard the femur was the most painful bone you could break. He knew me, and I could see that he was shaken to find out that I was the victim he'd been called to. He found blood in the snow. That, I hadn't seen yet. I saw that my ski pants had been torn near my right hip and I looked into the interior of my abdomen through two wounds that looked like side-by-side bullet holes. "Oh shit," I gasped. My breathing accelerated wildly.

As pitiful as I was, I felt sorry for him. He had a radio. "Get help," I said.

I was reliving a nightmare. The sequence was almost the same. Trauma and shock. Strapped to a backboard. The short jaunting sled ride to the Patrol Room. My clothes cut. The boots pried off. A doctor happened to be on site. He recommended a splint that strapped to my ankle at one end and wedged painfully into my groin at the other. This was supposed to stabilize the femur. The pressure left me groaning. Again, a half dozen people, people who knew me, worked furiously to help. There was the long drive to the hospital, this time in an ambulance. I was given a piece of soft wood to bite until I could get morphine, two hours away. At the hospital, I was rolled back and forth on a cold glass X-ray table. It wasn't the femur. It was the pelvis. The orthopedic surgeon said it was "comminuted." Comminuted means "reduced to minute particles, pulverized." As he put it, my pelvis was shattered into so many pieces he quit counting. He told me I'd be able to walk again but I wouldn't be running any marathons.

My courtship with Vreni became a series of conversations across bed sheets tarpolined over my toes and tucked under my arm pits. X-rays showed the imploded right crescent of my pelvis, hundreds of pieces floating in a collapsed white cloud. There was nothing to do but lie in bed and wait for the debris to petrify. I told Vreni a few stories. I told her this had happened before. I'd been bombing the mountain at exactly the same intersection of trails, hit a tree in almost exactly the same spot, and snapped both bones in my right leg at the boot top. I told her how my foot was detached except for the muscle and the skin, about the long months in casts, and more months of painful limping. I spent seven months in casts.[5] I told her

5 I had skied on one ski a couple of times, holding the heavy plaster cast up off the snow, and I skied the following winter, before the limp went away.

I'd broken my legs twice before I hit the first tree at Wolf Creek: one at eight, on my third day of skiing, the other six years later.

I confessed to her that at fourteen, I'd shoplifted a pair of ski boots. I'd wanted a green pair, but the ski shop salesman had fit me in a red pair. When no one was looking, I switched the boots in their boxes. As my father paid the cashier, I stacked the box with the rest of our gear. I was so flush with the success of the heist that a few days later, I rode my bicycle five miles back to the shop. In the dressing room, I managed to squeeze my Levis over a pair of stretch pants with rainbow side-stripes. I walked out of the store as casually as I could, my legs stiff. It was a hot day. I had to stand on the pedals because my knees wouldn't bend. By the time I got home, I was severely dehydrated. Over time, I knew the success of this theft would depend on remarkable lying: I told my mother my father bought the pants; I told my father my mother bought them. I depended on the fact that the two did not speak to each other since their divorce. Thanksgiving Day, my first day of skiing that season, I wore the green boots and the rainbow-striped pants. Near the end of the day, I fractured my right ankle. It was an odd accident. I never actually fell. A ski patrolman explained that the boots fit improperly. They buckled tightly around the top, but they were so loose over the instep. The ski caught an edge, the ankle rolled inside the boot, and the bone snapped. By the time I skied again, I'd outgrown those green boots.

I told her how in college, during a busy preseason sale, I swapped the $50 price tag off a pair of discount skis to a pair of Rossingol Haute Routes, which retailed for close to $300. Haute Routes were second only to Miller Softs as the premiere powder ski of the day. It was a little bit trickier than the green boots because the switch had to be made undetected amidst a crowd. I pretended I was interested in two sets of skis at the same time, moving back and forth between them on a long sales rack. Each time I visited the cheap skis, I peeled another centimeter of the price tag off until I got the whole thing. I stuck it to the inside of my thumb and hid it in my fist. Then, as I took a pair of Haute Routes off the rack and pretended I was testing the flex, I affixed the $50 tag over the $300 tag. As I checked out, I worried that the tag might curl up on a corner or that someone in the crowd had seen the whole thing. I was sweating.

I told her how I'd skied Vail on a counterfeit ticket. Kids in the neighborhood had stolen a laminating machine from the school and set up a photo plant in a bedroom, where they masterfully duplicated season passes, cutting and pasting Polaroids, recreating logos, inventing aliases. I told her how my "Ski-to-Fly" buddies and I were almost arrested by the State Patrol for jumping off the roof of a tunnel near the top of Wolf Creek Pass. So many people stopped to watch, traffic backed up for half a mile.[6] This was the same group of guys that hopped off chairlifts for the hell of it, stole firewood from grocery stores, and routinely shoplifted sandwiches from the ski area lunch counter.

I told her how I found one of my pals buck naked and in convulsions on the bathroom floor the morning after a ski area party. His body was stiff and cold, though he was drenched in a gastric sweat. His snow-white skin was opaque with spidery blue veins. He looked like he had been electrocuted and then preserved in a bath of antifreeze. His eyes were wide open, but he couldn't see. We wrestled his stiff body into a pair of pants, loaded him like plywood into the back of an old Datsun station wagon and set out for the hospital, a town away, first stopping to put more gas in the car. By the time he got to the hospital, he could walk a little. I got on one side of him and another friend got on the other and we helped him into the emergency room. A nurse approached. "We need a doctor," I said. I guess none of the three of us looked very good. She looked at us

6 The charge would have been "aiding the abetting of traffic on a state highway."

and asked, "Which one?" We paused for an awkward moment and then pointed to the overdose between us. "Him!" I said.

I think I told Vreni the story of how I stabbed a neighbor boy in the eye with an X-Acto blade when I was six, too. I was the first ski bum she'd ever met. She was a sweet Texas girl, a Christian. Before she met me, she thought skiing was about spring break and Young Life.

A ski patrolman was dispatched to the hospital to document the accident. I was asked to describe the wreck. Perhaps because of the morphine, I had trouble putting it into words. I asked for a pencil and paper and I was able to diagram the sequence. I remembered everything, except for the actual impact. Because it was a blank, I couldn't explain how I'd ended up backwards against the tree, or how my skis had come off, or what caused the puncture wounds.[7] The patrolman slipped the diagram into a file, impressed with its detail. I wasn't. The drawing was easy. It explained what happened, but it didn't explain why.

The day started out well. It was sunny, December 28th—peak of the holiday rush. I was in my sixth year as an instructor, which meant I was often assigned high-paying private lessons or the class of my choosing. The larger the class, the better the money, so when there weren't any privates around, I'd request the largest group, regardless of ability level. During a holiday, I'd sometimes take a group over a private lesson because the groups quickly develop camaraderie and they could be cajoled into buying several days of lessons—guaranteeing steady income for me.

Expert group lessons—called the "F" class—are almost never very large. Expert skiers, like advanced bowlers or advanced moun-

---

7 I figured out the punctures when I was given back my equipment. One ski pole was snapped in half. The hollow aluminum shaft snapped when it was crushed between my hip and the tree at the moment of impact. The sharp broken ends stabbed through my clothes and my skin.

taineers, seldom feel the need for a lesson. But on this day, a dozen people huddled under the "F" class sign—sporty types including skiers in one-piece suits that matched the color of their skis, a couple of college kids in athletic department sweatshirts, and an expertly outfitted teenage brother and sister. One woman, a middle-aged mom dressed in a powder blue jump suit and a ski hat with bunny ears, had been bringing her family to Wolf Creek for years. These skiers signed up so they could enjoy the privilege of cutting to the front of long lift lines. (It's a privilege that's included in the cost of any ski school lesson, no matter what your skiing level.) From my perspective, leading an "F" class was fun. I got to ski all over the mountain, and, if there were enough students, it paid as well as side-stepping around with beginners all day.[8] Plus, I got to cut lines, too. It's also true that having the seniority and the skills to take an expert class involved a measure of prestige. You had to be pretty cool to take an "F" class. (At least, I thought so.)

We started the bright morning with a wide slope on the right side of the mountain. A short way down, I stopped and huddled the class together. In instructorly tones, I explained to my students that I was acutely aware of what they'd paid for—make as many runs as possible. Because the mountain was busy, I asked that we gather as a group three or four times each run so that no one was left behind. I laid out a protocol: follow me, stop if I stop, give each other plenty of space, and at each stop I'd point out our next rendezvous. I looked back over my shoulder often. About half way across a long flat, a skier charged up behind me and passed. The sounds of his skis were troubling. The edges, scouring like an automobile skidding to a stop on a dirt road, indicated imbalance, a struggle verging out of control. (Did I hear him grunting with effort, too?) His tips clattered. Snow flumed like a comet from his

8 Teaching a full-day beginner class is the hardest work you'll ever do on a ski mountain.

flailing ski tails. His weight was back, his posture stiff, jack-knifed. His feet were held strenuously together. He had a definite—and outdated—version of style in mind.

I lengthened my turns to avoid him. The class followed, moving away as he heaved, turning by brute strength. His messy contrail clouded the slope. When he stopped, hockey-style, below me, I realized he was one of my students, the teenage kid with the sister. He was about fifteen, built solidly, like a budding linebacker. His bleached freckles were flush with competitive effort and acne. His grassy, rust-colored hair was clamped by the thick strap of his ski goggles. Before the rest of the class arrived, I skied in beside him. "Doug," I said, "You're a strong guy, and you have really good balance, but you're skiing a little bit beyond your abilities." I was trying to be professional, trying to imply. He squinted as he looked up the hill, watching the rest of the class swoop in around us. When the group was gathered, I smiled. "I forgot one rule I have in an expert class," I said. I smiled wider. "If you're skiing faster than me…"—half a dozen adults chuckled before I delivered the punch line—"you're skiing a *little too fast*." I then arranged the class putting the slowest skier, the mom with the bunny ears, directly behind me and positing Doug at the end of the line. I asked that everyone avoid passing the person immediately in front. I led the class to the bottom of the mountain. At the chairlift, we passed the jealous glares of a thousand skiers herded three abreast and five lines wide. All seemed well.

On the second run, I guided the group down the left side of the mountain, again skiing point-to-point to safe rendezvous. At each huddle, I pumped them with the promise of uninterrupted skiing, cutting lines, and touring the mountain with an instructor who could direct them to premium slopes and secret stashes. I hoped to keep the group together for as many days as possible. Two-thirds of the way down, I led the class onto a short slope that veered to the right and funneled between trees to a narrow road. I skied to the right of the run, so as not to wander out into the heart of the busy slope. After a few turns, I glanced over my right shoulder. To my surprise I saw Doug, airborne and headed my way. From the back of the line, he'd overtaken everyone else. In the air, he was out of balance, stiff, feet locked together. He looked like a calf roper vaulting out of his stirrups, red hair flaring. Through his tinted goggles I saw wide eyes. The instant his skis hit the snow, he accelerated. I looked down the hill. I heard his ski tips clatter behind me.

When someone is so close and coming from behind, there isn't much you can do. You have no way to predict whether moving to the left or the right will avoid or cause a collision. The trail narrowed. Doug was coming. I decided to let my skis run straight, accelerate, and move away from him—I hoped. It seemed to work, but then, out of the corner of my eye, Doug suddenly reappeared, to my left. In that same hockey-stop angle I'd seen him perform earlier, he had abruptly changed direction, toward me again. His hands windmilled. He desperately tried to stop, but his effort sent him into a long, reckless arc aimed at the bottle-neck where the trail went into the woods. I also headed for the bottle-neck, faster than I wanted to be going.

If I could have stopped, my life would be a different story. But stopping, though possible, suddenly wasn't an option. The mom in the pink bunny ears was right behind me, and the trail was too steep and too narrow to expect her to stop without rear-ending me. If I stopped, I was afraid she might veer into the trees. Skiing straight, I hoped I could speed ahead of Doug, but the moment he reappeared to my left, two skiers stepped out of the woods below, blocking the trail where it was narrowest. Apparently, they had not seen me or Doug coming. They moved like ducks in a shooting gallery, oblivious. I faded as far to the right as I could—closer and closer to the trees, faster and faster. They moved further and further to the right, cutting off any passage I might have through the bottle-neck. Meanwhile, Doug closed in like a meteor. I stood tall, pinched my shoulders and knees together, held my arms straight out as if I were going to fly through a turnstile.

Who knows what those two skiers thought as I whizzed past, almost brushing them. And who knows if their heads turned quickly enough to see Doug swoop in behind them, still keeled with the huge effort of his long, hard turn. If so, they saw him cutting toward me at a blind angle, like a line backer chasing a punt returner. Geometry took over. My straight path intersected with Doug's parabolic curve. I tried to push him away as we collided, but I bounced off like a billiard ball. The last thing I saw was the trunk of a tree inches from my face. Then blackness, silence. I awoke, paralyzed, squinting at that white, dreamlike sun, brighter than any sun ever. There was commotion around me. Someone asked what happened. Doug whimpered, "I hit him. I hit him."

I thought my drawing offered unequivocal proof of my faultlessness. The kid broke the protocol of the lesson, lost control, and couldn't stop or pass me safely—a multiple breach of skier responsibilities. Expert skiers know that skiers ahead of them are helpless and it's a "rule of the road" that the skier above must always avoid the skier below. I felt absolved. I was the one with a broken pelvis. The kid walked away unharmed. A friend, who had listened as I explained the key points to the patrolman, and who had heard the doctor tell me I would never run again, later told me he heard the kid's father was a doctor down in Waco. He said I should get a lawyer.

Perhaps I didn't get a lawyer because I knew how the accident happened, but that did not explain *why* it happened. Here's what really happened: a strong kid with good balance skiing beyond his abilities was powerless in the moments leading up to the crash. He was out of control. He had no choices. That's exactly what "out of control" means. A chain of cause-effect and gravity ruled his trajectory and speed. His was desperate, grasping. Somehow, thank God, he missed the two skiers waddling across the trail.[9] I, on the other hand, was not desperate, not completely. I had some control. I was aware of what was happening from beginning to end. In a few seconds I made a number of decisions. I was able to protect the woman skiing behind me. I was able to avoid the skiers in the bottle-neck. I almost avoided Doug. It could have been different. I could have stopped, veered into Doug's path, or used the skiers in the road as tackling dummies, and I probably would have come out better. Hurt maybe, but not crippled. More likely, whoever I hit would have ended up in the hospital.[10] I had some control.

In the coming months, this became important. As proud as I was of my diagram of the accident, its relevance faded. I came to see the chain of cause and effect that started long before Doug and I came together like two grains of sand converging in the neck of an hourglass. It started at the bottom of the mountain when I decided I was going to take an "F" class and have my fun while my fellow instructors slaved away with the holiday rush of beginners. I'd ignored something important. I saw that Doug was turned on by adrenaline rather than skill. I saw he was a menace. Why didn't I say: "Hey, Doug. You're out of control. If you want to stay in this class, slow down, now." Or better: "Hey, Doug. If you press forward with your knees, you can ski just as fast with more control." I was the *ski instructor*, after all. Why didn't I?

9 They were at least partly culpable. They also broke one of the maxims of "skier responsibility." Skiers merging onto trails are supposed to look above and yield to uphill traffic.

10 Although in the odd reality of ski collisions, the one with the most speed typically absorbs more of the impact than the one getting hit, so I probably would have been hurt, too.

The answer is simple. The stab of adrenaline already had its sharp, cold blade in me. I ate with it in me. I walked with it in me. I read with it in me. I dressed and undressed with it in me. I slept with it in my side, knowing an inopportune roll in the night would open a hole where subzero pain would rale. I was proud to live with high-risk everyday. It defined me. It was exactly why I was a thief. Stealing had little to do with the stuff I got. I loved the risk of stealing. I loved getting away with it. Skiing fulfilled the same obsession. Facing danger and getting away with it was deeply fulfilling. There was no drink or drug better than the rush of pure adrenaline. How could I see the dagger in Doug's side when I hadn't yet removed the broadsword from my own? I was a ski bum and proud of it. On the mountain, I lived by a ski bum's code: RULE #1—Don't get excited. RULE #2—Always pick up your paycheck; RULE #3—Try not to look like a hooked trout. He who hesitates is lost. A smart monkey doesn't monkey with another monkey's monkey. Don't drink too much and don't think too much, but don't stop drinking and don't stop thinking. Never go below six thousand feet. Ski to die, live to tell. I lived with enthusiasms and passion. Isn't that what Doug wanted? To be a ski bum, just like me—for a few days on Christmas vacation. I admired his noncompliance and mindless bliss. What right did I have to tell him to slow down? We were playing the same game against the same odds.

Except we weren't. My odds were worse. I didn't know it at the time, but I know now that every year the largest percentage of ski fatalities in Colorado occurs in the 25-34 age group. I was twenty-seven when I shattered my pelvis. If Doug had been eighteen, I guess you could say he was a little luckier than me. Skiers between eighteen and twenty-four account for about twenty-five percent of ski deaths. But at fifteen, his age group isn't even a mentionable statistic. Half of ski deaths in Colorado are skiers who hit trees.

It's hard now to imagine hitting that tree without feeling a magnetic attraction, like the inexplicable urge you feel when you look over the edge of a gigantic, deafening waterfall. It's hard now to imagine a life in which I didn't hit that tree. I think now of Doug as a coincidence, the tree as destiny. Before that day, I didn't know if I really cared whether I lived or died. After, I cared, and I knew I cared. For eight weeks I lay in a rented hospital bed in the corner of a friend's living room, only getting up to go to physical therapy. My physical therapist commented that she'd only seen one pack of X-rays thicker than mine. I was insulted. I asked who it was. She said the guy was a rodeo clown. That sounded like a cool career to me.

It was the winter of 1988. While the shards of my pelvis molded themselves back together, eleven skiers died in Colorado. Most of them hit trees. Their profiles fit me like a ski glove: young, fit, confident, male (almost eighty-five percent of skier deaths are males); expert skiers who skied fast at the edges of runs and inexplicably lost control for one moment and went into the trees. Most suffered massive head injuries.

It had been an average winter. I felt lucky.

I saw Doug the next season. I was teaching a small lesson toward the bottom of the mountain when another instructor skied up. Two skiers followed her. They were late, she said, and the ski school director asked her to help them find my class. I recognized Doug and his sister. His face went blank. Maybe mine did, too. It was plain that I never expected to see him again, and he had never expected to see me again. His mouth hung open, a black hole on his pale freckled face.

I turned to the girl who brought them. "I'm not taking him in my class." I said, and I skied away. Speeding to the bottom of the hill,

I found the ski school director. I said, "You can fire me right now if you want to, but I'm not taking that kid in my class."

"What kid?" he said.

"*What kid?*" I said. "That's the kid who *hit me*." I was furious.

My boss was flummoxed. "Do you really think he did it on purpose?" he asked.

"Does it matter?" I shot back.

By this time, the instructor sent to meet me had led my class plus Doug and his sister to the bottom. I'd already removed my skis. Heading for the lodge, I pointed at him and hissed, "Watch out for him."

As I simmered in a corner of the cafeteria, I felt a fire of shame and anger. By the end of the day, everyone else (except perhaps my deserted class) must have figured out what had happened. I wasn't fired. Nothing more was said. No apologies were made, nor demanded. To my knowledge, Doug and his family never returned to Wolf Creek. That day, I decided I had to leave the mountain.

Since I didn't know how to do anything else, it took me one more season to get off the mountain. I did modify my ski habits. I quit jumping off cornices and cliffs for the most part, and I took up ski racing instead. Though I decided I wanted to live, I still had lingering "issues," loose ends of my ski bum past, bad habits. Vreni sweetly suggested that maybe at twenty-eight it was time to quit pocketing cafeteria sandwiches in my ski school parka. She shook her head gently when I was almost fired for scalping lift tickets. She was miffed when, on the last day of my last season, I had to ask her to return a pair of Hart skis I'd given her for Valentine's Day. (That was a great gift—Hart skis on Valentine's.) I'd ordered them as demos from the manufacturer and never paid for them. I needed to return them because I was short paying off my area sales rep accounts. I'd given her a pair of red stretch pants and ski gloves that I needed back, too.[11]

At the time, I was also dodging a repo man and the IRS as I sold off personal items to raise money for a bankruptcy lawyer. She was exceptionally unimpressed when I fell off a bar stool at the end-of-the-season party. I had been doing the twist on it. She was right next to me when I lost my balance and crashed to the floor—on top of her. I spent the morning hours of that night sick with my head in her bathroom toilet. Before the snow melted from the peaks, she took her boys and moved back to Texas.

11 As an area sales representative for Hart Skis and Spyder Action Wear, I was provided with "free" skis and clothes and I "sold" skis and skiwear to ski area employees for promotional "pro deal" rates. In those days the accounting arrangements in the ski business were quite lax. Equipment could be ordered throughout the season, but the balance for the orders wasn't due until the end of the season. By season's end, I couldn't come up with the cash. I wasn't the only rep to abuse this system, and Hart and Spyder weren't the only losers. Promotional practices have since changed throughout the industry.

FIVE

REFUGEE

The bum in 'ski bum' comes from bummer, which rhymes with summer. It wasn't that I disliked summer; I resented it. I remembered the moment I discovered the word that exactly described my condition:

> **estivate** (esti·vāt) v.i. ·vat·ed, ·vat·ing 1. To pass the summer. 2.
> To pass the summer in a dormant state; said of certain animals.
> Compare HIBERNATE.

That was me. You could hardly find me in the summer. I'd work at some mundane job—groundskeeper, dishwasher, bike repairman, convenience store clerk, fish farmer—and ride and ride and ride my bike, waiting for winter. Half the time I was a transient, house sitting from one place to the next. When I got really bummed, I'd write a poem like this one:

STARE-OUT WITH THE MAN-IN-THE-MOON

The moon hangs in the sky
like a stone,

which it is.

I stare at it, like it's
a dented lotto ball,

which it isn't.

The moon stares back, like I'm
a dented lotto ball,

which I'm not.

The moon hangs in the sky
like a stone,

which it is.

I really liked thinking about line breaks and whether to capitalize the first letter of every line, or whether to capitalize at all.
Poets who refused to capitalize "I" always impressed me, but, of
course it had already been done. I really liked coming up with titles,
too. I took days to think of the right title. It soothed my mind. I
had great titles: "Halloween at the Country Bar," "One Thousand
Traces," "The Difference Between Smiling and Kafka," "Sky," "Sin
Offering," "Thunder, Respiration and Meaninglessnesses." Here's
another good one from that era, titled "I":

I

I am a shingle on a roof
nailed in my place
to be rained upon
snowed on
overlapped by other shingles
overlapping others

I am a wooden shingle
cracked by dry wind
faded by sun
nails driven through me
rust away

I fall with all other shingles
to rot on the ground
(like lost driftwood)
until the roof falls also

I wrote that one looking out my old bedroom window on a brief visit to my mother's. I'd just awakened from a nap and I looked out and there were all these gray shake shingles and it reminded me of a photograph my father had taken of a pile of old shingles beside an old mine shaft (he'd become a photographer after the divorce) and the poem just clicked. I wrote it in one sitting in about five minutes. It took a long time to type it because I made a lot of mistakes, and I was using a manual typewriter. (I didn't care much about typing. I got a D in the course, but that was before I had any idea that I'd have to type poems someday.) I decided to right justify it so the lines looked like shingles overlapping each other—sort of. I loved writing without punctuation. It was like not wearing underwear.

One more:

WATERCOLOR #1

When you split my heart,
be so kind as to use something spectacularly
silver and sharp, something silent and spinning
with teeth as clean as the blue, blue air,
something the knot of ribs won't pinch,
something that won't make ragged edges
where the blood comes flashing into the
blue, blue air—because when the
atriums and ventricles are opened like
an amphitheatre, I want to bleed the
clear, dry, arching colors—both sky
and stone—of the high painted deserts
at the last of the last of evenings.

That's a one sentence poem. I read somewhere that every person on the planet says something everyday at least once a day that no one, in all time, has ever said before, and I derived a deep sense of purpose from the thought that I might be saying something unique more than once a day and I was writing it down.

If I really, really got into a funk, I would write a short story, but I had to be pretty bummed out for that and it had to be a short-short story because of the typing thing. Here's one that pretty much summed up how I felt about summer:

LOVE AFFAIR

You live in a place where it hardly ever rains. One day you wake up; it's raining like a Chinese painting, and you know it will last all day. It happens to be your day off, so you can do anything you want, or nothing.

You put on your raincoat and hat and walk down to Brodie's Supermarket and buy two navel oranges. After you buy the oranges, you have twenty-five cents left in your pocket, exactly twenty-five cents. You decide to go to the post office and get a newspaper from the machine out front, so you can go home and eat the navel oranges and lay the paper across your lap, which you hardly every do, because you hardly ever get a day off, and it hardly ever rains, and the news is never new anyway.

Still, you love the thought of turning the pages of the newspaper and eating the navel oranges, because it is raining and it is your day off and you can do anything you want to, or nothing.

It's Monday. The newspaper in the machine is Sunday's. But you aren't thinking. You just want to hold the paper and unfold it across your lap where it will catch the juice spurting from the navel oranges you're peeling.

You aren't thinking. You watch the rain shatter into patterns on the wet streets. You put your only quarter into the machine and tug. It doesn't open. Then you notice the machine is still half-full of Sunday papers. It's Monday. Newspapers on Sunday are exactly seventy-five cents. Newspapers on Monday are exactly twenty-five cents.

You want to kick the hell out of that newspaper machine, and you would if it wasn't raining like a Chinese painting and people weren't running in and out of the post office. You tug on the machine again, but the paper inside is Sunday's.

You walk back to your apartment in the rain that will last all day, shattering itself on the wet streets. You peel the navel oranges and eat them, standing over the sink in case the juice squirts.

> Then you sit by the window and think about cleaning up
> your apartment while your raincoat and your hat dry out,
> because it's your day off and you can do anything you want,
> or nothing.

Of course, everyone who read that said, why didn't you just go read the paper at the local coffee shop? Or why didn't you go in the post office and see if you could get your money back? Some people said why didn't you just buy one orange? One guy said, you know if you weren't such a ski bum and you had a better job, you could have had the paper delivered. I protested that I could hardly type, and it was a pretty good story, considering. They were impressed by that, but, still they just didn't get it. The whole point was, none of those things crossed my mind. I couldn't think straight. It was summer and I was *estivating*.

I didn't write much, really. It was just something to do in the summer. If I had any gas in the tank of my convertible, I'd just get in and go. I had a favorite spot, the Great Sand Dunes. They were only an hour away.

I'd been to the dunes when I was a kid. My family moved to Colorado from Philadelphia when I was eight, and my father, as peripatetic a man as I ever knew, was eager to explore the state. Every weekend was an expedition, part of his lifelong mission to get his sons outside. Medano Creek was high that year. I was wearing a knee-high plaster cast on my broken left leg,[12] so my father carried me across on his back. It must have been early June. Along with my three brothers, we climbed toward the first sand peak, what I thought was the top. At first, I sprinted on all fours, dragging the cast like a lame crab.

Half way to the top it was already full of sand and heavy. I climbed slower and slower. My father and my brothers waited. I soon discovered that we had scaled but a ripple of an ocean. I saw

12 I'd broken my leg in the spring on my third day of skiing ever.

wave upon wave beyond and above. I don't remember if that's when the tears started, or if they came after the wind picked up. Shortly, it was blowing hard enough to rip a phone book in half. It seemed like all that kept me anchored was the weight of the cast. Miserable, angry, half-blinded, and crawling on my belly, I never reached the summit. I remember the descent as worse than the climb and got no satisfaction from it. I was, however, oddly proud when, a week later, the orthopedic surgeon cut off my cast and found enough sand to start a respectable ant farm.

In summer, I loved to go to the dunes at night. Once I went out with some friends to fly kites in the moonlight. But usually, I went alone. I'd run up the mountains of moonlit sand, leaving a trail of clothes behind me. On top, I ran from dune to dune. I remember the bluish skin of the formations, gargantuan and anthropomorphic. I remember the sand's touch. Soft winds passed near the surface like breath. A few handfuls down, moist sand radiated with human warmth. Once, high up—high enough that I could see the scattered lights of tiny, distant towns—I was startled by a coyote. "What the hell are you doing here?" I said out loud, surprised by the sound of my own voice. I crouched down. We looked at each other without moving for a long time. Then, the wind shifted slightly and she trotted into a shadow below. I ran on across her tracks, sand flying from my feet as I climbed, adrenaline coursing in my arms.

That may have been the night I could see the moon in the rear-view mirror of the convertible for the whole drive out. I adjusted the side-view radically so I could see the moon in it, too. I was taken away, seduced, by the sparse desert wilderness. I felt a primeval yearning—a madness—for the sand itself, as if I could become one with it. In those nights, undetected and naked and run down to exhaustion, utterly alone, in the most limbic of states—the small, empty cry of the desert aroused my deepest unnamed hungers.

Out there, the commingling of inner and outer desolation meant something. What? I didn't know. Maybe out there, I first saw that my fury and my fleeing were irreconcilable.

Any one of those nights could have lasted forty or four hundred or four thousand years. Time disappeared. While I was out there my impetuous, needy, wild heart felt the wind blowing through it. It seems silly now, but without that desperate, wounded heart, those nights would have just been blank, forgettable nights and the moon would still be just a stone in the sky.

SIX

ANOTHER HEART

It took a year-and-a-half, three thousand dollars in long distance
bills, several trips to Texas, and a proposal to get Vreni back to
Colorado. She knew she was coming back to marry an ex-ski bum,
but I'd gone straight. I'd bought car insurance, earned a Colorado
Teaching Certificate, and settled into respectable work, teaching
literature, writing, speech, and drama to the sons and daughters of
dry land farmers and migrants at a high school in a Dust Bowl town.
It was barely in Colorado, just twenty miles from the Kansas border
and not too far from the highest point in Oklahoma. We rented a
house in the next town west, a hot, high plains crossroads—even
lower than the highest point in Oklahoma, thus violating the ski
bum's six thousand feet rule—flanked by two sizable stockyards,
a nine-hole golf course, and a minimum wage plant that built high
tech passenger buses. The most popular restaurant in town was the
truck stop, where the salad bar was spread out in an old buckboard
wagon.

It was a two hour drive to the sight of the tip of the nearest peak,
and another hour and a half to the nearest ski area, which was
closed most of the time for lack of snow. About five hours away, a
modest family ski area on a high pass in the Sawatch Range offered

a great family season pass. We asked the boys if they would rather take a trip to Disney World or ski. They elected skiing, so every winter Friday night, we'd pack our 1985 VW Jetta, make the long drive, sleep in cheap hotels, and ski from opening to closing Saturday and Sunday. Vreni often drove on Sunday nights while the boys did homework and I graded papers.

I remembered Wolf Creek with mixed emotions. It was the place I'd formed my greatest friendships and met Vreni. But it was also my Normandy—the site of a difficult emotional and physical passage. Confident our toughest struggles were past, Vreni and the boys and I lived happily, day by day, paycheck to paycheck. Ski racing became a new passion. It was actually safer than the kind of skiing I'd done before. The speeds were slower, and racing was safer in two other ways: race courses are purposely directed *away* from trees, and race training is closed to the public—no one to run into you.

But after a year, the long weekend commute caught up to me. I announced that I was done skiing. Working, working out five days a week, all the driving—much less the hours of hard practice on the hill—was just too much. I was tired all the time. I couldn't motivate myself to get back in the car. As a family, we all agreed to take a break for a year.

This was the first sign that something was seriously wrong.

Since the little town we lived in didn't have a cardiologist, we drove three hours to Denver. We liked the enormous aquarium stocked with exotic blue fish that dominated the waiting room. The receptionists and nurses seemed animated. Most of the patients sitting around were older than I was by thirty or forty years. The cardiologist's personal office wasn't much bigger than a cubicle at a car dealer, but it was comfortable and sunny. Vreni sat beside me and we waited. Though we'd spent only part of an afternoon with him, we liked him. His grey tweedy moustache matched his jacket. His blue eyes were inviting and energetic. Like a friendly stage hand, he had circulated us to and from waiting rooms and labs. We chatted about skiing. He complained about a bum knee and joshed that life wasn't worth living if you couldn't ski trees and bumps. I agreed that bumps were fun. But I told him trees scared me.

The treadmill test had not gone well. As I started to jog, one white coated technician yelled to another, "Get him off!" And then yelled at me: "GET OFF!" I was confused and offended. I was thirty-three. They knew I'd been a ski racer, a ski instructor, and a river guide. They knew I could ride a bike for a hundred miles without stopping and I had run 5Ks in under twenty minutes. I was ready to run on that treadmill all day long. But I was done before I broke a sweat. The electrode tabs pasted to my chest were still cold.

In the office, the cardiologist explained. It was that old murmur I'd been ignoring. The condition, a congenital valve defect, had worsened. A narrowing had narrowed even more. Instead of all the exercising I had done increasing the heart's volume and power, my heart had accomplished the hard work by pumping faster, danger-ously faster. When my heart rate jumped up on the treadmill, the technicians feared I might have an attack.

We viewed a cloudy, grey video tape of my beating heart squirming like a landed fish. A white spot mid-screen indicated calcification around the aortic valve, caused by excessive turbu-lence. I'd need open heart surgery, to implant a prosthetic valve, probably within a year. Vreni held her breath. My hand moved to her knee. All we had been through—the shattered pelvis, the long separation, her big move back. It was hard enough for us, and harder on the kids. We'd been married less than two years. Now this. I couldn't believe it.

She knew the back story. A murmur had been detected when I was eleven. I was forced to quit football, soccer, basketball, ski racing. Things I was good at. Eventually baseball, which I loved, went by the wayside, too. Oddly, I was allowed to play tennis. I hated it. I practiced and played in a fugue of foul-mouthed rages—smashing rackets. By my senior year, I'd quit the sport. At twenty-one, I'd undergone a heart catheterization. The murmur was diagnosed as aortic stenosis, a congenital defect of the aortic valve that progressively restricted blood flow to the aorta, the body's largest vein. There was talk about "fixing" it, someday, maybe in my fifties. The news didn't mean much to me. I hadn't had any symptoms. After high school I'd moved to the high country and done what I wanted. In the summers, I rode my wobbly ten-speed up the steep mountain passes just so I could race cars on the way down. All I had for a helmet was a baseball cap turned backwards. In the winter, I skied like a madman.

I was famous among a small circle of like-minded friends, guys who drank the same cheap beer and also hucked themselves off cornices and cliffs. They marveled at my complete and quick recoveries. They watched me cut off my own casts and remove my own stitches. Like them I was tough, strong, a rugged individual. A few of them knew that secretly I'd accepted I might die any day anyway, because of the heart condition, and if I had to go I was determined to have fun. The same guys teased me relentlessly when I met Vreni and the boys. They nicknamed me 'Daddy.'

I guess fifty seemed like an eternity away and I never bothered to ask how a thing like aortic stenosis would be "fixed." I don't remember open heart surgery being mentioned.

Vreni knew all that.

In the bright office, my life was changing radically, again. After the surgery, I'd have to take powerful anticoagulants for the rest of my life to prevent blood clots and stroke. I'd be a pharmaceutical hemophiliac—restricted again. Simple accidents that most people shake off could have potentially fatal complications. Activities that could lead to broken bones, contusions, deep lacerations, or head injuries were forbidden.

No soccer with the kids, no football. The kids and I had been taking Tae Kwon Do together. No more rodeo clown for me. The drug meant weird, small changes, too. Alcohol and Vitamin K interacted with it, which meant less beer and spinach. Aspirin and ibuprofen thinned blood and might result in internal bleeding. Decongestants raised blood pressure, adding to the danger of stroke.

I was frightened, by the surgery itself, and by so many changes coming all at once. Would I be allowed to ski? I reminded the cardiologist that life isn't worth much if you can't ski trees and bumps. He smiled and suggested I buy a helmet. Rather than resentful, I felt inspired, privileged, lucky. I'd had a bum heart all my life and I wanted it fixed. Vreni and the boys gave me reason to live. Even rodeo clowns have to retire sometime.

I felt very lucky when I found out about the tell-tale symptom for my condition: sudden death. It almost happened that way. Just a few weeks after I'd abandoned skiing for the season, I collapsed playing basketball. My chest went rigid as a cinder block. My breathing seized. My vision tunneled as I dropped. Every element of my being burned white hot. I lay on the cement not knowing if my heart would start again. It—the end—is stunningly quick and simple. Your heart stops. The air around you becomes inert. Oxygen looms, sticks to your skin, floats before your eyes, invisible and meaningless. The weight of the air pushes you down. It seems just as impossible that your heart will start again as it was for it to stop in the first place. That's it. It's over. *You* are done. The end.

I'd been dodging bullets for years. Less dramatic symptoms had come up before, but I kept them to myself. I thought I'd had too much caffeine or it was allergies.

I wanted surgery right away, but we had to wait. When the shortness of breath I'd experienced with exercise turned up during normal activity, it would be time, a sign that the calcification had worsened and the valve had narrowed even more. Then, the risks of postponing would outweigh the risk of surgery. I was told that a prosthetic heart valve would enable my heart to strengthen itself. It would learn to pump stronger and pump more volume rather than adjusting to heavy work loads with dangerous jumps in heart rate. I was hopeful, optimistic. For the time being I waited. I was prescribed a heart rate monitor and assigned a maximum heart rate of 120. One-twenty ruled my life.

That winter was a cold one on the high plains. Streets were snow packed. The boys were getting older and learning basketball. I dribbled around a little, but there was always that number: 120. (When Vreni and I discovered that making love broke 120, we agreed that some things were worth dying for.) I showed the boys a plastic model of the valve I would receive and explained how it worked. The blood pumped from my heart, pushed through it and then closed it automatically, like French doors opening and closing in the wind.

Late in the spring, an old friend was passing through Colorado and he talked me into meeting him for a half day of skiing. I wore the heart monitor. If leaps in heart rate were dangerous, it's a miracle skiing hadn't killed me years before. My heart rate would jump to 175 half way through an intermediate run. I told my buddy I wasn't supposed to go over 120 and I showed him the display on the wristwatch. He just laughed. He said, "If you were going to die, you would have died a long time ago. Just ski and forget about it." Then he said I might as well get in a few turns before I died on the table.

Summer came. I could hardly ride a bike without going over 120. To kill time, I went to auctions and developed a small collection of antique skis. A fellow high school teacher had a wife who had just opened a massage parlor that sold aromatherapy products, body lotions, and a line of concentrated liquid vitamins. He kept hinting that I should try the vitamins. When I explained that aortic stenosis is different than high cholesterol, he said maybe the vitamins might swoosh the calcium off the valve.

The success rates for valve implants are high, but I prayed. I wrote every friend I could find and asked them to pray for me. I never prayed for a miracle directly, but one night I walked to the edge of town and I looked out into the dark and the stars and I prayed that if God decided I should be healed, that would be fine. I promised him all the credit.

Not long after that I was reading 1 Samuel for the first time when I came upon the chapter in which Samuel, the prophet who was called "a Seer," brings the "word of God" to Saul, a tall young man, and a good man, from Israel's smallest tribe. Saul doesn't yet know he is destined to be the first king of all the tribes of Israel. Among other things, Samuel promises Saul that he "shalt be turned into another man," and moments later "God gave him *another heart.*" I could hardly believe it when I read that: another heart. It was exactly what I needed. Did God give him a completely new heart? Not a figurative change of heart, but a completely new heart? Why not? If God gave me my faulty heart at birth, he could give me another heart later. The words—*God gave him another heart*—seemed written for me. It couldn't be a coincidence—me reading the Bible for the first time and finding those words. I was glad to find out that God was in the heart business.

Nine months after the treadmill test, I stood backstage of the high school theatre surrounded by anxious, eager students. We waited under hot stage lights. My forehead beaded with sweat. I felt tension in my chest, like a belt tightening under my armpits. I couldn't catch a full breath. As I stepped out to introduce the show, I asked one of the bigger students in the cast to wait for me behind the curtain, just in case I tipped over. It's just stage fright, he said. But I don't get stage fright. It was time.

On the morning of December 15, 1993, the big news story in Denver was a shooting spree. The night before, a nineteen-year-old boy wearing a Raiders jacket and black gloves with the knuckles cut out walked into a suburban pizzeria and started shooting people in the head. He had been fired from the restaurant several months earlier because he refused to stay to the end of his shift. He promised to get even. Earlier in the evening, he had stopped by the restaurant for a ham and cheese sandwich. He asked which manager was on duty. He came back at closing time with a gun. By the time I entered the operating room, the fourth of five victims was dead. While Vreni, the boys, her mother, my mother, my father, two of my brothers, my father-in-law, and several friends waited, details emerged. One young man, a dishwasher who had had the job just two weeks, survived. Shot in the jaw, he fell to the floor. He played dead until the shooter went into the manager's office. Then he ran. It was his day off, but he had taken someone's shift for extra Christmas money. His wife, who also worked at the restaurant, had stayed home with their baby. One boy was a high school wrestler and coached kids in gymnastics. His mother allowed his organs to be donated. One girl, a high school senior, enjoyed singing. She'd been standing beside the cashier, a nineteen-year-old girl who had recently written a letter to a friend about the violence in the city. *Be happy you don't live here. So many kids with guns, tons of people dying. I haven't personally known anyone who died yet, but I always know someone who did know them.* Her geometry teacher said she was the kind of girl who would touch the future with her successes. The manager shot in the office was not the manager who had fired the boy. She and her husband had moved to Colorado from California because they were tired of the senseless, random violence there. He said they just wanted a simple life. She'd had the job less than two months. The gunman's mother lived nearby. When she heard the news, she ran to the pizzeria. She knew all the victims. As she embraced the mother of one of the girls, someone told her the shooter was her son. The governor called for cooperation with religious organizations and asked businesses to help idle youths find jobs. A University of Colorado psychiatrist said the factors in a mass shooting are complex and blamed the gun. You don't hear about drive-by poisonings, he said. A police psychiatrist said when it happens in a place like that, a place that is supposed to be safe for kids, it makes the whole world seem unsafe. A high school principal said the things that were important yesterday don't seem so important today. The gunman's younger brother worked at the restaurant but was not on duty that night. Another employee had left the restaurant fifteen minutes before the shooting.

As an open heart patient, innumerable procedures, things you would never dream of doing to yourself, are performed on your body. Needles as wide as soda straws are shoved into the boniest corners of your wrists. Tubes dangle from them for days. More "bee sting" needles come and go, poked into the soft nooks of your elbows, and more dangling tubes administer unpronounceable drugs that you would never otherwise take or pronounce.

You are rolled to places you could easily walk. You lie on gurneys shoved to the side of hallways and stare at ceiling tiles with disorienting pinprick and hole punch patterns (that same ceiling tile you find in principals' offices, police stations, and above dentists' chairs). Immediately after a pre-operative sedative, which melts your worries like warm syrup, the most delicate and intimate of your appendages gets nudged around. You might, if you are still awake, realize that your pubic hairs are being shaved by a very nice, very gentle, very professional guy in cold latex gloves and a heavenly blue skull cap.

Of the surgery itself, you will remember nothing except a dreamless sleep, black as construction paper. As you sleep, a vacuum cleaner hose is jammed down your throat. A person you met the day before (soon to be your hero) slices your chest open from just below your Adam's apple to just above your belly button. Your sternum is chopped in half with a circular saw that would serve as well to build a backyard birdhouse. Your ribs are winched open like a set of storm shutters. Your lumpy, red and blue heart is filleted. More tubes grow from your chest. When you wake up, you look like a greenhouse irrigation system.

When I awakened, I couldn't tell how long I'd been under. It seemed like a few seconds had passed. I felt normal—no pain, none at all. Even with the respirator still in and with my arms restrained, I felt great. I scribbled 'NO PAIN KILLERS!' on a notepad. I sincerely believed it. A guy as tough as I was didn't need painkillers. Open heart surgery was easy! My friend Sam—a skinny black-haired kid who would eventually go to mime school in Paris—believed me. He announced to everyone in the waiting room that I'd had open heart surgery without painkillers. They all laughed.

Once the respirator was out, I gulped the sweetest, coldest grape juice I'd ever tasted. My throat was dry and sore, and I was famished. I asked for more. At the exact moment I saw the bottom of the second cup, I puked grape juice everywhere. As nurses cleaned me up, I saw myself for the first time. My chest was laced together like an over-inflated, old football. Large metal staples held me together. I could see what lay ahead wasn't going to be easy. It was going to hurt.

In my hospital room, a Mend-a-Heart volunteer (a sixty-year-old man who was an open heart survivor) gave me an odd hand-sewn pillow about the size of a Pringles can, powder blue, with a felt Valentine heart stitched to it. He explained that my sternum was wired together inside and it was going to hurt like hell when I coughed, laughed or, God forbid, sneezed. Every open heart patient gets a little pillow. The pillow was to brace against my chest in these emergencies. I thought he was joking. I laughed, reflexively pinning the pillow to my chest. The pain was like lightning. From that moment, I did everything with one hand. My pillow was in the other.[13]

I was surprised that my father spent a lot of time at the hospital. He had had a by-pass surgery a few years earlier and I suppose he felt we were members of the same brotherhood. Mostly he read, until I complained that I couldn't sleep because the sound of turning pages was too loud. Everything seemed amplified. A gurgling machine beside my bed was hooked up to most of my tubes. Another machine flashed numbers and beeped at random. Nurses had squeaky shoes. Vreni piled pillows on my head so I could sleep. Time was an eternity. I had a nurse drape a towel over the wall clock. Besides making the time crawl by, it reminded me of my old morphine nightmares. Those memories might have been what I was thinking of the night I tried to quit my pain killers. I thought the sooner I was off them, the sooner I could leave. I spent hours resisting the sensation that a scalding plow was surging through my chest before I begged for relief.

Vreni stayed with me through the first few nights, in a little bed set up in the corner. My family visited. Old friends from high school visited. Other friends traveled hundreds of miles to see me. Some were obviously shocked. I was so helpless, so dependent, so

13 Years later, I handed mine down to a neighbor who was going in for an open heart procedure.

deflated. Every face was a warm reunion.

I found out that I was down the hall from a seventy-two-year-old man who'd had the same surgery. Also on the floor was a woman in her mid-thirties who'd received a liver transplant. A lifelong diabetic, she was given a pager when she moved to the top of the organ list. She'd rushed to the hospital. She was in surgery at the same time I was. The liver she'd waited so long for came from one of the kids murdered at the pizzeria.

I couldn't wait to see the boys. Vreni ushered them in. They were so good, like they were coming to church. Ryan, his thick comical hair parted and combed, was tall enough to see over the sheets. He smiled and put his hand gently on me, his big green eyes feeling my pain. At our wedding, he'd read a poem I wrote for Vreni. He'd never slept without the light on, until he hucked his first cornice. That night, he told Vreni: "You can turn the light off, Mom. Once you jump off a cornice, sleeping in the dark isn't that big of a deal." Matt was still a little boy of consistently unastonished expression despite round, blushed cheeks. He'd wetted down and tugged his blond hair neat and flat. He'd been the ring bearer at the wedding. He grabbed the bed rail with one hand and handed up a small box with the other. Vreni told me he'd picked it out himself and bought it with his own money. He nodded seriously.

Inside the box was a beveled mirror about the size of a postcard. Decaled vertically on the mirror was a short poem. To read the poem you had to look at yourself in the mirror. The poem read:

> *For always being there*
> *to care.*
> *Always trying*
> *to be fair…*
> *For every piece*
> *of good advice.*
> *Every quiet sacrifice…*
> *For being strong*

and gentle, too.
Most of all for being you—
Thanks, Dad.

The day I was released, I asked the cardiologist what I was allowed to do. He said, do whatever you want. Have a beer, run a marathon. He assured me there was nothing I could do to hurt the valve. It wouldn't pop out, as I feared. He said I could throw the heart monitor away. No more 120.

We all stayed in my mother's apartment in Denver for a few days. I slept on the couch so I could sit up. I didn't feel great. I couldn't eat much, and I felt nauseated. About a week after the surgery, I was able to walk to a nearby strip mall. The winter sun felt as bright as paradise. I decided to get a haircut. It was something I could do while resting a little, and I wouldn't have to carry anything home. I thought the hair stylist was one of the kindest people I'd ever met. It seemed like a miracle that there were people on the planet who were nice enough to cut your hair *for* you. Life was beautiful.

I barely made it back to the apartment. Short of breath, I felt like I'd eaten a Thanksgiving dinner and then run a marathon. I collapsed on the couch and slept. Late that night I became ill, so sick that as I sat on the stool I threw up into the bathtub. Everything smelled fecal, like bad meat, and it looked like wet coffee grounds, gallons of it. I was in there for what seemed like hours, my body convulsing violently. I worried I'd wake everyone up. All the while, I held that little cough pillow to my throbbing sternum like it was a lifejacket in a hurricane. Miraculously, I didn't wake anyone. Finally, I took a shower, cleaned the bathroom, including rinsing out several towels, and went back to the couch. I figured all open heart patients went through it. Somebody guts you and you feel horrible for a couple of weeks. I thought about that poor seventy-two-year-old man.

The next day, after a check up and an X-ray, Vreni and the boys and I were packing when the phone rang. It was the surgeon. He wanted me back at the hospital, immediately. There, X-rays showed blood was leaking from my heart. The sack surrounding it had filled. My right lung had collapsed under the pressure. That's why I couldn't breathe, why the nausea. The coffee grounds in the bathtub—that was blood. The anticoagulants were partly responsible.

I was told I needed another surgery, to drain the blood, insert drainage tubes and re-inflate the lung. I said no. I'd spent nine months psyching up for open heart surgery. And I did it. I'd been split open like a piece of firewood. I couldn't do it again. They left me to talk with Vreni. I covered my face with one hand and the other held that damn little pillow to my heaving chest. I was afraid they would open me up again. I was afraid I wouldn't make it. I told her how weak I felt. I remembered the blackness, the blank nothingness. I told her I didn't feel lucky anymore. A few hours later, I was sedated, rolling into another operating room, and counting backwards: one hundred, ninety-nine, ninety-eight, ninety....

Four more days. Four nights. The greenhouse hoses sprouted, again. Tiny tubes hung like spaghetti, again. The incessant gurgling. Flashing numbers. Beeps. Squeaky shoes. A pile of pillows. A towel draped over a clock. My little stained Valentine pillow. The lung was okay, but on the morning after, a stranger, my surgeon's partner, dropped in. My surgeon was out of town, *skiing*. The bleeding was still worrisome. The sub announced he was going to insert an extra drainage tube. A nurse ripped open a large package, producing a long, clear hose while the doctor applied a local anesthesia. About midway up my right rib cage, with what looked like an X-Acto blade, he made an incision the size of a coin slot. The opening turned to red lips. The doctor and the nurse manned the hose. I braced, one hand gripping a rail behind my head, the other clutching my Mend-a-Heart pillow to my chest staples. They came at me like a crashing wave. The wires that held my cracked sternum together strained. I felt the hose slither inside me. I closed my eyes, watched the lightning, and roared my protests. They shoved again. I opened my eyes and roared a stream of oaths that were more personal and specific. Quickly, it was over and I lay in my cold sweaty sheets. The doctor said he was sorry it had to be a substitute. I told him I didn't blame him. I asked where my surgeon was skiing. Did he have a pager? I just wanted to ski a few friendly runs and then direct him to the nearest cliff. The sub laughed.

We finally made it home after New Year's. It was hard to look at myself in the mirror. My body was pale and bloated. I looked like I'd floated up from the bottom of some scummy harbor, several days after I'd lost a fight with an axe murderer. The internal bleeding was still a concern. I weighed myself daily. If I gained suddenly, it meant that sack was filling up again. I walked half a block one day, a block the next. In between, I slept. I walked every day until I could walk a mile, then two. I hated walking. Eighty-year-olds walked. Four miles was the goal. I worked up to it. I still hated walking, but I decided being eighty might not be all that bad.

My heart was still loose from its pericardial anchors and it banged around like a Superball in a recipe box. The new valve clicked loudly. The pain in my tender sternum and ribs was constant. Even when I was exhausted, I couldn't sleep for long. The Superball and the clicking and the pain—plowing and plowing— were too much. Awake in the dark, I'd squeeze the little blue pillow to my chest and reach for Vreni. All I wanted was to be able to put a hand on her. Not to wake her. I just wanted to touch her, and feel her breathe, and know what sleep felt like.

SEVEN

THE LAST BUFFALO

Though I hated walking, I was motivated. Once I could walk four miles, I was cleared to do anything I wanted. When I hit the goal, I vowed I'd never walk again. It was boring, doubly boring out on the plains. The town we lived in was so small there was no way to cover four miles without passing two cemeteries. All those headstones gave me too much pause for thought. I could hear the dead whispering—as if I'd been so close I was already part of their gossip. "Not yet," I'd say, as I walked past, "not yet."

It took six weeks to work up to four miles. By then my sternum had healed, with the wires still inside. (On a chest X-ray it looks like I'm still held together with bread twisters.) It would be a while before I could do a push up, but I started riding my bike and doing sit ups. I wanted to ski before the season ended. Little did I know, I was getting back into shape so I could almost die one more time.

Vreni and the boys had a different spring break than I did, so I set out by myself driving straight west and stopping at the first ski area I could find. It was a beautiful little place beside the Sangre de Cristo's Spanish Peaks. The slopes snaked between bare aspen trees. The view from the top was stunning, looking east over the plains for a hundred miles. To the west, a range rose above timberline, the white edge leaning against a lily blue sky. I brought a brand new pair of skis for the occasion. It was sunny and warm. The slopes were groomed like soft mattresses. I skied fast, thrilled that I remembered how to do it, thrilled that I was doing it at all. My heart pounded like a brand new bass drum.

Everyone on the hill seemed just as excited as I was, like it was their first day out since open heart surgery. I rode the chairlift with a local ski patroller.

"Isn't this great?" she said.

"This is great!" I said.

"Can you believe it snowed?" she said.

"We're lucky, aren't we?" I said. I told her I was impressed with her enthusiasm. I knew from experience that when you work at a ski area a little burn out sets in around spring break.

"I haven't had time to get burned out," she said. "This is our first day." She explained that the area hadn't received snow all season long until two days before. A storm dumped three feet. It took a day to pack runs and call employees in, so it was literally the first day of the season for everyone.[14]

Somehow, I survived the skiing and drove on, deeper into the mountains, over a nearby pass and out onto the floor of a high, grand valley. I was headed for a friend's in a small town on the backside of the Sangres, where the peaks are Teton-like. I took a short cut that passed close to the Great Sand Dunes, my old haunt. It was a moonless night. Except for the cutout of the mountains against the stars I couldn't see the dunes, but I could feel the massive presence of the sand. The headlights seemed to push the darkness away like a plow pushing deep black snow. The stars along the top of the windshield splattered against the glass like glittering mosquitoes. A

14 The weather was so nice, the snow melted in two days and the area had to close down again. Eventually, bankruptcy closed the place for good.

million miles from the nearest cop, I jetted across the desert floor, drunk with the afterglow of skiing.

My mind drifted from pleasant thought to pleasant thought. Wasn't I the luckiest man on the planet? I'd dodged death again, three times in less than one year: heart attack, open heart surgery, and then critical bleeding and a collapsed lung. Everything common—the road, the stars, driving—had the intensity and newness of a miracle. I was so happy I didn't even care if I could ski bumps and trees. I'd ski on a doormat if it had snow, and be ecstatic.

Then the road ahead became oddly dark. The stars on the horizon were blotted out. The high beams seemed to disappear into a black hole. By the time I figured out there was something— something huge—in the road, all I could do was veer. In the flash of the headlights, I saw an immense, beastly profile coming over the hood. One big, wide black eye, as black as obsidian, stared at me through the windshield. It was a buffalo, its hoary head so close I thought it was going to crash through the glass. The head reeled away from the light, as if a sword had been swung at it. I heard and felt two solid thunks—thunk/thunk—on the side of the car as it hurtled into the ditch.

I took my foot off the gas, but I was still going sixty or seventy miles per hour through Chico bushes, rocks, and sand. It felt like a herd of longhorns was charging under the floor board. All I could think was that I was off the road and if I hit the brakes, I'd be hopelessly stuck in the middle of nowhere. The wheel tried to jerk out of my hands. I wrestled to steer and punched the gas wondering if the next chico would have a giant rock behind it. Miraculously, the car hopped out of the ditch. All four tires seemed to hit the road at once. I was able to stop the car.

My heart pounded hard in my throat, like a new bass drum. My eyes bulged with every beat. My kidneys flooded with hot, pounding blood. My back turned to stone. My legs froze. My arms were still flexed, hands squeezing against the steering wheel. I yowled: HWOOOOOO! I yawped: HWOOOWHOOOO! I laughed and I laughed and I laughed. I yowled and I yawped again and I laughed some more.

I got out of the car. Dust was still settling. I figured I had been in the ditch for about two or three hundred yards. I ran back down the road, into the darkness. There was nothing but me and the cold desert air and the stars, down to the horizon in one direction and ripped by jagged peaks in the other. Then it crossed my mind that an angry buffalo might charge. What the hell was I doing chasing a buffalo in the dark? I sprinted back to the car, giggling breathlessly. I turned around and around, the headlights probing out into the shrubland, but it was gone.

The next day, I inspected the car. The driver's side mirror was crushed. I found a scar on the panel behind the driver's side rear window. That was the second thunk. The mirror smacked the poor buffalo in the nose. Thunk one. Her head spun and a horn butted the side of the car. Thunk two. I shook my head in disbelief. That had to be the luckiest buffalo on the planet.

EIGHT

INSTANT KARMA: CONFESSIONS
OF A SKI BUM, PART III

After three years in Southeastern Colorado, Vreni and I decided we'd had enough. As nice as the people were, the heat and the plains were too much. We were mountain lovers. We lined up summer jobs guiding rafts. The job included housing for us and the kids. After that, we had no concrete plan. We just wanted to get back to the San Juans, where we'd met. I had a small retirement account, and we figured if we made $10,000, we could scratch through a year. Vreni wanted to go back to college. Her loans would help out. We laughed at how foolish we were. But we shared the dream. After open heart surgery, a little financial hardship didn't seem like a big deal.

We moved to a tiny town of about six hundred year-round residents on the headwaters of the Rio Grande. We were back above 6,000 feet again, 8,880 to be exact. It was a quaint ex-silver camp, nested in a corner-pocket canyon at the foot of snowy wilderness ranges—spectacular. The place had nearly gone bust in the mid-'80s and recovered by adapting to summer tourism, selling its pristine scenery, fly fishing, art galleries, T-shirt shops, a unique summer repertory theater, and a free-for-all Fourth of July party.

The housing fell through and we ended up camping out of our van on the banks of the river for the summer. The boys loved it. In the fall, we lucked out and found a cheap rental. Vreni and I commuted three days a week to the regional college, eighty miles away. She went to classes while I taught writing. The rest of the week we worked in town. She made coffee and sandwiches in a local café while I picked up a few hours in the town's mom & pop outdoor store. In time, I settled into steady seasonal work, alternating the writing instruction in fall and winter with a job as a ranch hand in the spring and summer.[15] Within a year, I'd cashed in my retirement and we bought a tatty little house south of town. When she finished her degree, Vreni was hired to teach at the local elementary.

Except for a hiccup a few years after the heart surgery—a minor stroke that put me in the hospital for some tests—and a few minor injuries, my health was good. I'd given up most everything that might seriously endanger me, except skiing. This was a conscious bargain of the sort that every true addict understands. I narrowed my thrill seeking to ski racing, and defined "ski racing" very narrowly. I specialized in slalom. It's the slowest form of racing, characterized by short, sharp, turns. Picture a Hotwheels track in which there are no straight-aways. The emphasis is on skill rather than all out speed, so, I rationalized, I was minimizing my chances of traumatic injuries. Because slalom technique required a skier to go through and over gates, it had an attraction for someone like me—that is, for someone who was a pharmaceutical hemophiliac. Every competitor took advantage of plastic body armor, literally from head to toe. I could protect myself from serious bruising. So, picture Rollerblading down the Hotwheels track in full paintball gear.

15 Even this came about because of skiing. The guy I worked for was an old friend from Wolf Creek.

For the first couple of seasons, I couldn't afford lift tickets, gas, or a potential breakdown in my aging car, so I mail ordered two dozen hinged racing gates. On free afternoons, I'd drive to the foothills, and my dog would watch me side-step up and down a slope, packing the snow with my skis. The next day, I'd lug the gates up the hill, set up a short course and hike and ski five or six practice runs. The training was decidedly subpar.[16] It showed. When I finally scraped up the money to go race for a weekend, I fell the first day—finishing dead last. The next day, I was disqualified for missing a gate.[17] Still, I was elated. I was thirty-six. I was alive. I was on the mountain. It sure beat intensive care and puking grape juice all over your gashed chest.

Eventually, our budget improved and we again bought season passes to our old family favorite in the Sawatch Range, now three hours away. Wolf Creek was only forty minutes, but aside from the harsh memories of my crashes (and exorbitant season pass prices), it seemed a bad vibe persisted.

Once, Vreni and I were skiing for the base area there on a wide beginner run at the end of a quiet weekday. A frenzied patrol-man—Gil, a holdout from the old days—waved us down as we came up on a gentle knoll. Approaching fifty, Gil still had the lean frame of a carpenter, dark flapped sunglasses permanently tabbed to his tan face. Still out of breath from scolding two other skiers, he popped out of his skis and started across the hill toward us. We were already stopped, but he hollered, "Slow down!"

"Sorry Gil," I apologized. I didn't want to make trouble, whatever we'd done.

Gil said, "The speed limit on this run is five miles per hour."

16 The snow was far too soft to replicate an actual race course, and I spent far more energy on hiking than I did skiing.
17 The races were at Beaver Creek, Colorado, part of the Rocky Mountain Masters Series, which provides top-flight age-group racing for competitors from age 21-80.

"I didn't know that," I said. "I must have missed a sign." I'm sure I was smiling. Skiing five miles an hour is an absurdity.

"Well, there's no sign," he said. "It's ski area policy. Five miles per hour, and I have to enforce it."

I pointed out, politely—Vreni for a witness—that I'd been skiing well to the side of the trail, as far from anyone else as I could get. I admitted that I was skiing faster than most do on a beginner run, but, I pointed out, I also stopped the instant he waved me down. This, I reminded Gil, demonstrated that I was skiing in control—as per the Skier Responsibility Code.[18] "Maybe you're right, Gil," I conceded. "Maybe I shouldn't even be skiing over here." I explained that Vreni and I were on our way home, it was late, and we just wanted to ski something easy to the bottom.

"You're skiing too fast," he persisted. "I could take your ticket right now."

I apologized again.

He lectured on.

I interrupted him when a couple of skiers crept into view from above. Their pace was typical and controlled. "Those skiers are going fifteen miles per hour. Are you going to bust them?"

Gil was undeterred. "The speed limit on this run is five miles per hour. There's no sign. It's ski area policy. Five miles per hour, and I have to enforce it. You're skiing too fast. I could take your ticket right now. *Five miles per hour!*" As he spoke his ski gloves waved, the fingers signing as if I were deaf.

18 THE SKIER RESPONSIBILITY CODE:
- Skiers should ski under control so they can stop and avoid other skiers and objects.
- Downhill skiers should make certain that when they are overtaking a skier, they are able to stay out of the path of that skier.
- When entering a trail or starting down hill, yield to others. Look uphill first.
- Keep off closed trails and posted areas and observe all posted signs.
- Do not stop where you obstruct a trail and are not visible.
- All skiers shall use devices to prevent runaway skis.

I held my gloves up in surrender. "Okay. You're right, Gil," I said. "Would you please radio for a toboggan for me."

He stopped. He wiped a glove across his mouth. He scanned from my boots to my helmet. For the moment, he was arrested in deep and sincere professional apprehension. "Are you hurt?" he asked.

"No," I said, "but I don't think I can ski five miles per hour, and I need a ride to the bottom."

"Well, five miles per hour is the speed limit here."

"Gil, I know I can't ski five miles an hour. And even if I did, it would be dark by the time I got to the bottom of the mountain." That finally got him. He grinned. I assured him that I would ski to the bottom as slowly as I could.

The next day, I sent him a card reiterating my apologies.

A couple of months after the ski area closed, I found out my name had been added to the Wolf Creek LIST. The LIST was a compilation of skiers whose behavior presumably poses a threat. The LIST, I learned, was posted in the confines of the Wolf Creek Ski Patrol Room. The LIST was unofficial and secret, but it was consequential. I discovered, having my name on it meant that one more "infraction" would result in banishment from the ski area... *for life*! I ran into Gil in town that summer. We talked. No hard feelings, he said. He was just doing his job, and he'd had a nerve racking day by the time he'd waved me down.

I asked, "Since there are no hard feelings, would you please take my name off the LIST?"

Gil's dark sunglasses turned to me, an insinuating beetle-black glare. It was as if I'd discovered the Mason's secret handshake. "No hard feelings," he said. "But once you're on, no one can take you off. I can't take you off."

I shrugged. "You put me on. We agree, it's no big deal now, and it really wasn't even a big deal at the time. Just take my name off."

The conversation became circular. Jokingly, I mentioned Kafka. I mentioned Orwell. I mentioned the Nazis. The sidewalk was busy with summer tourists, and Gil became increasingly tense. Exasperated, he said. "The speed limit on that run is five miles per hour. There's no sign. It's ski area policy. Five miles per hour, and I have to enforce it. You were skiing too fast. I could have taken your ticket. *Five miles per hour!*"

Gil's heated reaction caused me to inject "the LIST" into every sentence I uttered, until I thought he might actually put a finger to his mouth and shush me. Finally, laughing, I said, "Is *this* an infraction, Gil? If we have a conversation on a street corner in July, and you decide you don't like it, can you ban me from the ski area for life? And what if I'm banned? What if I show up at the ticket office in a Nixon mask? Are they not going to sell me a ticket? Is Idi Amin on the LIST? Is the Unibomber on the LIST? Is Milosevic on the LIST? If the pope were skiing six miles per hour, would you put him on the LIST?"

Gil laughed. I laughed, and we both walked away shaking our heads.

Our conversation on the street was the last time I saw Gil. What Gil didn't know was that I knew Wolf Creek Ski Area never had a policy, written or understood, that the speed limit on that run was five miles per hour. In his agitated state, he'd made that fact up. So there was no real infraction. But I was on the LIST anyway. He's since retired. Presumably my name remains on the LIST—and will even after he dies, and will after I die. My only consolation is that perhaps cards of apology are tacked up beside the names of the guilty. I pray that those who might judge my future "infractions" will exercise compassion.

Another thing Gil didn't know: I actually did keep a Nixon mask in the glove compartment of my car.

Bad vibes. Sometimes I got hassled at Wolf Creek before I even got my skis on. Once I tried to park at the back of the parking lot. A guy in moon boots and a parka that looked like a sleeping bag rushed me. He waved a red pennant at me and pointed his opposite mitten toward the front row. As I rolled down my window, his breath steamed heavily into a walkie talkie harnessed to his chest like a bionic heart. "Got him!" he huffed. The kid wore a blue nametag that said "ALF." There was no explaining that all I wanted was to park near the entrance because I planned to leave early. "Go to the front or get towed," he barked. I noticed Alf had ingrown eyelashes, so I didn't argue. I headed for the front. Over my shoulder, I yelled, "I have a Nixon mask, Alf!"

Months later, I figured things had cooled down, and I conspicuously avoided Alf by heading for the 4WD lot above the lodge. There, I was waved down by another flag-toting sleeping bag. "Got him," he huffed into his chest as I rolled the window down. Earnest was his name. "This is *four-wheel-drive* parking!" Earnest said. He was a large, young man, thick beard tipped with a Barbie doll braid. He had strong looking ivory-black teeth set in wide magenta gums. "Yeah?" I said. He said, "Your vehicle is *all-wheel-drive*! Go to the lower parking lot or be towed!" I was really miffed. I said, "You know, Earnest, I have ..."

"Yeah, we know," he interrupted. "You have a Nixon mask. Big hooty." He stepped in front of the car and directed me away with his red flag.

Despite the hassles, and the old traumas, sometimes I missed working on the mountain. I missed the bitter, clear mornings when the sun glared on the snow white as copy paper and the air smelled like icy tonic water. I missed the fat crows that used to hector me from the tree tops. I missed being on the divide, where the air was as blue as the oceans astronauts saw from space. I missed skipping lunch—lunchtime was for skiing—and coming home to a cabin where you could feel the wind blowing between the logs for a dinner of peanut butter sandwiches and cheap beer. I missed rooms full of friends—ski bums, too—jamming to LPs of the Moody Blues, Pat Benatar, and John Cougar. I missed the '63 VW bug we used to take up the pass packed with six or seven people. I missed making turns in deep, pristine snow alongside guys I absolutely trusted. Mostly, it was that, the camaraderie. There's nothing like a friend on the mountain. You work together, play together, share the turns of the day and the turns of life.

I really missed sweep. Sweep is the term for the clearing of the mountain at the end of the day. As the chairlifts shut down, patrolmen and instructors huddled at the top. Sometimes we'd all cram into a little top shack, waiting to give the last skiers a head start. A supervisor assigned each person a run. It was our job to ski that run and make sure that everyone made it off the mountain. We all had a favorite run we would either request or trade for. Once assigned, you were handed a thin board a little bit larger than a business size envelope. A lanyard was laced through a hole in the board. You hung it around your neck and took off. A trail map was glued to the board. Your route was highlighted. You made your way chanting "Sweep! Last run!" down the hill and into the trees. Included in the route were specific points where you stopped, located the instructor or the patrolman sweeping a nearby run, and acknowledged each other with a wave. Then you proceeded to the next appointed "wave-off" chanting "Sweep! Last Run!"

I loved "sweep" because I loved the feeling of being on a deserted mountain. I'm sure it reminded me of when my brothers and I were kids and we hid from the sweepers, then skied down behind them. I loved the quiet slopes in the shadows of evening, the mountain contours losing their shapes in flannel blue light. I loved the depth of the suddenly indigo sky and the last geometric brilliance of the sun on the southern pyramids of the San Juans. I loved the lonely chanting intonations echoing from the hollows and trees. "Sweep! Last run!"

I still love being last. I love the sweet regret of it.[19]

19 Sweep was a volunteer duty for which ski instructors were paid $4. I volunteered nearly every day of my career. It is a bygone tradition. Wolf Creek now has enough full-time pro patrolmen to handle the task.

NINE

WAVE-OFF

Anyone who lives above six thousand feet anywhere in the Northern hemisphere knows Andy Gray. I mean, you probably know someone a lot like Andy Gray. He's exactly the kind of guy you might become friends with if you met on a mountain, the kind of guy you'd realized you liked a lot more than you thought you did once he was gone. I met him by accident. It was the summer of 1991. I was guiding rafts on the Upper Rio Grande when he ambled into town just down off the Continental Divide Trail. He wore a backpack that weighed more than he did and carried a shoulder-strap stench to match.

He clumped into the office of Mountain Man Tours Rafting and commenced to swapping river stories with The Mountain Woman. He had the look of a Dickens extra: Irish street urchin grown to stable boy, bird boned, rusty-headed, a thinning face with equally thinning profile, mousey nose, ears stuffed with straw. You almost expected him to come out with a cockney accent. His pale eyes, set sharply to rocky rise lines, were forged with self-reliance. He was quiet, forthright when he did speak.

It turned out he had done some guiding on the Colorado out

"near Utah." Always short a guide (or about to fire one[20]), The Mountain Woman hired him on the spot. He probably didn't want the job, but he was only nineteen or twenty, and maybe at that time guiding a raft was the only thing he knew how to do. She handed him the keys to a rickety Dodge van and sent him down to the river bank to help shuttle rafts and clients back to town. The guides, myself included, found him waiting on a rock under the bridge at the take-out. Leather brimmed hat pre-salted over Jeremiah Johnson locks, he was ready to work.

"The Mountain Woman said to say she sent me," he announced politely as he grabbed bow lines and helped stack rafts on trailers. It seemed like he knew what he was doing.

"Who are you?" my boss, Greg Coln, a.k.a. The Mountain Man, asked when he finally noticed the kid behind the steering wheel of the van. In those days, Coln wore full rendezvous leathers—medicine bag tucked into his Cavalry belt on one side and a harpoon-sized Buck knife on the other. He was a trek-scrawned, grubstaking, yellow-haired, Tennessee vagabond who, years back, had also hiked down off the Divide. I think he was suspicious of Andy's rawhide hat and wiry backcountry build, both so closely resembling his own. Who would presume to be a mountain man in the audience of *The* Mountain Man?

"Andy," Andy answered, matter-of-fact, as if he were *The* Andy Man—land ethicist, eco-monk, solo-trekker, Outward Bound-geek.

The next day, Andy followed me down slow water as we floated eight-man rafts filled to the gunwales with clients from the Amarillo Square Dance Club. Without the soothing current and the vaulting, cut-cliff views of the Grande's palisade walls, the situation would have been Andy's version of hell. He was a gritty, tethered nomad—part Sherpa, part ski bum, part river rat, part

20 She fired me twice!

monkeywrencher, part handyman. Like most full-timers above six thousand feet, he had a near-religious reverence for the rocks, the sky, the water, the snow, and a near-revolutionary suspicion of tourists. There he was, stuck for hours on a raft with a huddle of cheerful, fat, red faced Texans asking questions like "What do y'all do in the winter?" and "How cold is this here river?"

People wanted to take him in. The Mountain Man found him a trailer to rent, paid the deposit, and bought him two sacks of groceries. Yet it was hard to get close to Andy. He had old backcountry habits. One spring, while on a week-long run of the Green River, Coln put him in charge of the supply raft, which meant he also maintained the expedition's "groover," a portable latrine. As Master of the Groover, Andy's duty was to set it up and break it down. On the first evening of the trip, Coln stopped at a sandy beach and set up a kitchen and a fire as the rest of the group set up camp. Coln was turning steaks on the grill when Andy pulled the groover up to the fire ring, flipped the lid, dropped his pants and began to... groove. Coln shook his head in disbelief, looked up from the fire and said, in his wizened Tennessee drawl, "Andy, do you really think that I want to sit here and watch you groove while I'm cooking the steak I'm about to eat?" Andy replied, "Oh. I thought this was a good spot. It's warm," and he continued to...groove. Coln became more specific, "Andy, I do *not* want to sit here turning the steaks I'm about to eat and watch you *groove*." Calmly, he instructed Andy to pull his pants up and drag the groover to the bushes. "Oh. Okay," Andy said.

By that time, Andy had become somewhat of a Mini-Mountain Man, a protégé. He added a modest feather to the band of his hat, and an imposing knife to his leather belt. Leather and bead-braid necklaces hung in his unbuttoned felt shirts. He even harvested a fuzzy Fu Manchu. As remarkable as his version of The Mountain

Man was, it is groundbreaking that Coln adopted some of Andy's style, most notably by incorporating shorts into his river apparel. Hitherto, no one had ever seen the Mountain Man's skinny legs. He also adopted Andy's footwear: clutter-soled hiking boots over sagging wool socks. This is how it became evident that people liked Andy, by a detectable but undeclared influence.

Andy's indelible mark on me came in the form of his oft used, favorite, and annoyingly frequent shibboleth. *Actually*, not Danger, was Andy Gray's middle name. As in:

> Me: Whoa! Did you see that Andy? I just ran over another chipmunk.

> Andy: I did see that. Actually, what you just ran over is—actually, *was*—a California Gray Squirrel.

> Me: If they're California Gray Squirrels, how come everyone calls them chipmunks, Andy? And how come they aren't gray and how come they aren't in California, Andy?'

> Andy: Actually, I don't know how that got started.

No doubt, when Andy was stuck for hours on a raft with a huddle of cheerful, fat, red faced Texans, he exacted subtle revenge, peppering tourists with his subduing *actuallys: Actually, that's a lodge pole pine, not a spruce. Actually, the Rio Grande is the third longest river in the United States, not America—especially if you take into consideration South America.* Ad nauseam, ad infinitum, et al., et Andy. To this day, I can't utter an "actually," or listen to someone else say it without thinking of him…and annoying myself a little bit.

Handy Dandy Andy Man made a base and found a place for himself in San Juans. We knew little of his background and it seemed almost irrelevant, psychologically or practically. He never asked anyone else about theirs. He took people at face value, and he took mountain living the same way, doing what everyone in a tiny mountain town does to get by, which is whatever it takes. He parked a tiny fifth-wheel at the trailer park, equipped it with a wood stove, skirted it with hay bales and scrummed up a couple of vicious, barking dogs on chains. He hauled wood slabs from the mill in a fraudulently licensed, no turn signal/no brake light pickup bed trailer and mostly kept to himself. He guided rafts, taught skiing, hucked cappuccinos at the coffee house, patched plumbing, fenced, and hauled trash. Somehow, he got himself a Colorado Teaching Certificate, and subbed at the school. They say the kids liked him. Andy fit in just fine.

One winter, he bought a plow for his dual-wheeled flatbed Toyota, which went well with the snow chains, shovels, Hi-Lift jacks, and sand bags already hanging from the homemade bed rails. I hired him to do my drive. We actually filled out an official looking contract. When a big front hit in January, piling snow thigh deep, he never showed up. I left a message on his machine. Late that night, he returned my call. I asked, "Are you calling to tell me you're on the way over, Andy?"

"Actually...no. I'm calling to tell you I'm not coming," he said. He said my driveway was too hard with this much snow and he'd saved it for last, but it got too late. *Of course*, I thought, as I shoveled the heavy snow in the dark. *You can't have a contract with Andy.*

He finally settled into the cheapest rental in town, a mustard-colored, fort-styled little stucco locals called "The Alamo." He slapped together a cave of plywood scraps and hay bails for the dogs. One dog, Bear, was a white northern breed with a matted coat that rode her back like a sheepskin saddle blanket. The other, Taco Monster, was the biggest German Shepherd I'd ever seen. Part of the reason Andy moved out of the RV park was the dogs kept chewing through the metal door of his fifth wheel. The yard turned into clawed dirt.

Sometimes I wished he drank so I could break a friendly Budweiser over his whiskered nose. The kid had the impertinence of a master's candidate fresh out of orals. I could tell when he thought I was stupid. He'd get a straight lipped, know-it-all smirk on his face. But I used to drop in on the coffee house—a funky, rough-cut espresso/latte joint with a wood stove and a poetry loft—just to see if he was around and what he was thinking. As he hit his late twenties, I noticed that more and more often he didn't just seem to know what he was talking about; he actually knew what he was talking about. It never got heated, but he had no tolerance for the confabulations of a figurative thinker like me. In the middle of what I thought was a friendly conversation on wolf reintroduction or old growth timber harvests or forest service land swaps, he'd simply burn me with the facts, like so: "Actually, reintroduction isn't really an option. It's a requirement of the Endangered Species Act. It's actually the law." One time, over I don't remember what, he caught me in a bad inaccuracy, and I blurted, "Andy, you are *actually* one irritating son-of-a-bitch." He was flattered. "Thank you!" he said. It was probably that day that I decided I actually liked him, the way you like a little brother who's always in your way on the stairs.

Andy and I never skied together. But I did see Andy ski once. I'd tagged along with a pack of Wolf Creek ski instructors out to Montezuma Bowl, the plunging undercup of twelve thousand foot Alberta Peak. Chutes streaked down the mountain wall like white war paint. The ski conditions were typical: post-storm crud that had been skied to an al dente wicker, still soft enough that knee-deep blocks splashed open like loose hay bales. One at a time, we all scribbled our little ant farm paths to the bottom, stacking short turns tight as puka shells. Andy came last. His turns swaled the entire width of a chute. I could see why he'd waited. He needed the rest of us out of the way. At the end of the first turn, he half-hopped, changed direction, hooked his skis back into the checkered snow and eyelinered across the entire concave of the slope—like a skateboarder accelerating in the deep end of an empty swimming pool. Another hop brought him to rest in the avalanche tailings where the group had bunched up to bitch about the chunky conditions.

I was impressed. Once on the boards, Andy—land-ethicist, eco-wonk, solo-trekker, Outward Bound-geek—had an inner Errol Flynn. Those long, pendulous garlands weren't bail-outs. They were high speed, chin-out, suspension bridge, Dick Durrance, lace-'em-up, cable-binding, Tuckerman's Ravine classics. The way Andy skied it, the inconsistent snow looked like good surf. I couldn't help thinking, *Why didn't I do that?*

"Nice turns, Andy," I said. "All three."

"Actually, four," Andy said, "if you include stopping."

Andy never shed the habits of a restless Ute, and he covered approximately the same territory. Give him a day or a weekend or a month off, and he was gone. The Rockies were his trap line, and he had to go check it out. Ask where he'd been, and you got a two word answer.

"Near Boulder."

"Near Taos."

"Near Utah."

"Near Utah?" I'd ask.

"Near Utah," he nodded.

"How near Utah?"

"Not actually in Utah," he said.

His trips didn't coincide with concerts or festivals or any seasonal high country migrations. He returned on schedule, or not, with nary a story—bullshit or otherwise—no pictures. He'd just been somewhere, alone—somewhere not many people go at a time when not many people were there. I guess to talk about it would ruin it.

Eventually, Andy left. I'm not sure why. It was just time. Vagabond-age. He needed gas money, so he sold me his Handy Dandy Andy pickup bed trailer for fifty bucks. He parked the fifth-wheel in my backyard. I knew he wasn't coming back when he sent me the title with a note saying I could sell it.

Two years later, Andy showed up. Vreni and I ran into him dur-ing intermission at the repertory theater in the middle of August. He wore a surprising and durable smile. He'd settled in Telluride, and he was eager to introduce his surprised, smiling, Telluride bride-to-be. A Handy Dandy Andy gal, she was—a sunny, sturdy blonde, about three inches taller than he. He didn't want her to meet anyone in particular. He wanted her to meet everyone. She was easy to meet, an affable girl. They were obviously both love-struck. She clung to his arm, like a morning sun to a mountainside. He gave me his phone number and invited me to ski Telluride. For the next month, his old friends quietly celebrated the new happily-ever-Andy. "Did you see Andy?" one would say to the other. The other would say, "Actually, I did."

Too abruptly—early in October—we learned Andy had died. He wasn't even thirty. He was hit head-on by a drunk driving on a revoked license. The extreme, violent twist contrasted cruelly with the leave-no-trace, low-impact philosophy that inspired his life. I'd have preferred it if he'd been pinned by a shifting rock in a desolate canyon outside the soul of nowhere. At least he died like the restless, Ute-spirit he was: going somewhere to check out those trap lines. His fiancé later told me he was headed out someplace not many people go at a time when he knew no one was there. She didn't know exactly where. He'd said was headed for someplace near Utah.

TEN

INSTANT KARMA: CONFESSIONS
OF A SKI BUM, PART IV

I've lived my whole life with the sense that something particularly fine was about to happen to me—something that would solve all my problems and make life simple and clear. My earliest memories are filled with visions of this simplicity and clarity. Even when the path ahead seemed tangled and dark, I felt the promise of a full future and I knew that all I had to do was wait. Thus, everything I've ever done was temporary, part-time—what I had to do until the expected came to pass. I never had to wait long. I always got what I wanted, because what I was waiting for came once a year, every year: winter.[21]

At the instant the first September cold front crosses Colorado, I can't think straight. The coming of winter has profound overtones. As with no other season and no other experience, except perhaps sex, it distorts my grasp of reality. In winter, my fantasies seem profoundly real. The unstable structures of the season collapse on my psyche, and the rest is a slide away from normal life toward a dreamy neverland. In winter, it's easy to give up on everything, everything I've planned, everything I've accomplished, everything

21 The inspiration for this passage can be found in A. R. Luria's study on memory, *The Mind of a Mnemonist.*

I believe. In the face of the first snowflake, I see the face of God, and in those who follow lesser but infinite gods, bringing mundane existence to a freezing halt, and I feel convincingly that I've arrived in exactly the place at exactly the time I was meant to be.

Like gout, my *raison d'etre* swells again. I have numbness in my upper thighs. The microfibers of my calves twitch. My coccyx tightens like a mealworm. My feet become achy and distended. My forehead is lacquered with sweat while the eave of my brain stem drips with icicles. I hallucinate. The bed sheets are infested with spiders. My memory fixates on distorted visions, like a damaged DVD's broken digital images graphing the screen into calico. The blank squares of the malfunction flood with a crossword puzzle of flashbacks.

Why not live this way? Wait, for what comes. "Deal with brute nature," as Thoreau said. "Be cold and hungry and weary." Make up your own names for each type of snow you ski, as the French, in the midst of revolution, made a name for each day. Wait!—I say—for nothing is finer than the arrival of what you have always been waiting for.

Just forty minutes from my home, Wolf Creek typically opens in October, earlier than any other ski area within a hundred and fifty miles. Since I'm not a season ticket holder, this is a torturous fact. It's like being kept inside for recess and then forced to watch everyone else play outside the classroom window. Several seasons back, Wolf Creek opened even earlier than usual. With an acceptable base already on the ground, local forecasts soon called for a big storm. Heavy rain in Southern California was a precursor to several days of snow in the San Juans. On a Friday morning it started. Flakes the size of potato chips descended like dragon flies, and snow stacked up in my front yard. I suffered symptoms: sweaty palms, accelerated heart rate, dizziness, dry mouth. Before my wife had pulled out of the driveway on her way to work, I was calling in sick.

To calm my jitters, I set up my ski tuning bench, filed the edges and waxed the bases of my favorite pair of skis. I slipped an 8" blue tang, hard chromed Mill Bastard File (made in Finland) into a file guide and filed until the beveled metal edges were sharp enough to whittle fern-like shavings from the pink smiles of my fingernails. I polished the edges with 400 grit Silicon Carbide "Electro-Coated" sandpaper, the kind used to buff finishes on automobiles. The metal shone like the matching blades of a broadsword. Using an old iron—set to "wool"—and a 60 gram block of Norwegian-made Low Fluorocarbon/Graphite ski wax.[22] I dripped a bead along the bottoms of the skis, then laid the iron flat on the plastic bases and spread the wax as it melted. The aroma was soothing, hints of vanilla and cinnamon. A trace of white smoke rose from the tip of the iron.

A half day will be plenty, I told myself. *What's a credit card for?*

Half day tickets went on sale at 12:30. I left the house at 11:30. Plenty of time, even if the pass was snowy. Ten minutes from Wolf Creek, a line of cars was stopped for construction. I'd forgotten about the delays. I waited. I opened the window, laid my head out. Flakes sizzled on my forehead like sprites of water dancing on a hot pancake griddle. Every minute was a minute of skiing, gone. Snow accumulated on the wet road. I tapped my fingers on the steering wheel. I knew what I was missing: avalanche bowls, knife ridges, cornices. It mattered not that the snow could be junk—heavy, wet stuff that stopped you dead in your tracks, or sucked you under like quicksand. And what if I was missing thirty-three inches of dandelion fluff that flared from behind you like a contrail? My half day was disappearing. Old neurotic grudges percolated. I couldn't get it out of my head that Wolf Creek wouldn't take a local check

22 $22 for 2.1 oz.!

on "Local's Day." Finally, traffic moved. The storm thickened as the car climbed. By the time I got to the parking lot, snow was exploding from the trees.

Twenty minutes later, I dropped my skis onto the white lint. I snapped into my bindings. I paused under chairlift #1. It was 12:30 sharp. Half-day tickets were on sale. Snow swirled. A lone chair-lift operator dug like a badger in the pit beyond the loading ramp. Empty chairs passed over him. The storm glowered. This was just the introduction, the polite oriental bow, the first lean of it. The core was coming. When the storm really hit in a few hours, it would collapse like a falling drunk, right in Wolf Creek's lap. The storm would last days. The pit would be filled with thirty inches of snow by morning and that poor guy would be digging again—head down, shoulders tight, goggles fogged. For some reason, he had no partner, which meant he had no time to check tickets.

When two skiers slid into line, he scrambled from the pit and tilted the chair as they sat down. They rose slowly into the squall. A few more skiers came along. He didn't check their tickets either. My boot liners warmed around my ankles. I smelled the wind, a salty chlorophyll tincture. The zipping, cold snowflakes tasted galvanized. My blood flowed steadily, peacefully. I visualized the blazing, white morass of the summit. My brain flat-lined. The ski patrol would be preoccupied with raising fences, signs and tower pads to keep them from getting buried, visibility so poor they wouldn't be able to tell from a distance who had tickets and who didn't. Convinced I wouldn't be caught, I slid into the empty lift line. As I stepped into the loading zone, the operator dumped his shovel and swam out of the pit. I shifted both poles to my left hand and looked over my right shoulder. The operator stood to my right anticipating the coming chair. I saw that he was a she, red hair sprouting from her blue hood. The wind howled, throwing a shawl of snow between us.

"I hear it's really going to dump!" I hollered.

"Yah! Dude," she smacked her fat mittens together and stamped her pack boots, "Eight foot swells off Malibu, dude. They're talking feet!"

"Cool," I said. She grabbed the sidebar brusquely and tilted the chair as I sat.

The chair swung and yawed from its slacking cable. By the time I was to the top, snow filled my lap. I waved to the kid in the top shack. He wore a black beanie tugged down on headphones. He was rolling a cigarette behind his large window. As I slid down the unloading ramp, I was engulfed by new gusts of snow. The storm was opalescent. Every object I might have otherwise recognized—a safety fence, an island of trees, a drift—molted in blurry, white shadows. The diffused light straddled everything. I was alone at the top of the mountain, flush with triumph. I'd beaten the gods and the odds again. I'd survived another summer. Still alive. And, I was skiing for free. *I'll never die in winter,* I thought.

The first run—MY FIRST RUN OF THE NEW SEASON!—felt like a bronc ride. I couldn't see the humps and potholes on the trail. At the bottom, I shuffled into the loading zone. The operator stuffed her scoop shovel in a drift and waded out of the pit again.

"It's really dumping!" I hollered.

She smacked her fat mittens together and stamped her boots, "Yah! Dude. It's been raining in Laguna for three days. They're talking feet!"

"Cool," I said.

She tilted the chair for me.

I remembered to buckle my boots for my second run. I scratched a film of ice from my goggle lenses. They immediately iced up again. I looked into the white maw through two small portals. I sensed the evolution of the front. When you've lived in the mountains long enough, the birthplace and life of storms are disclosed by the doorways through which they appear. Years of recognizing patterns and cycles—feeling the weight of the sky, breathing humidity or lack of it, shivering at sudden gradients of temperature, sniffing micro-dusts from the jet stream—feeds your hunches. It smells like it's going to snow, and it does. Over the years, your hunches are verified and honed, tested and calibrated, against the collective archive of the community. In high country, the weather is the real news. Volatile and fickle, it's more entertaining than politics, and more far-reaching.

Thus, the hypnotic attraction of a snow storm. For its relatively short duration—a few hours, a few days—it rules. Each storm has a body, idiosyncrasies, personality. Years hence, we remember the gravest blizzards like a good scare, a thrill. We gossip about them, intimately, as if an axe murderer came knocking door to door late one night and we all saw him through the keyhole, saw how fat and bearded and lurching he was. We smelled his whiskey breath streaming under our thresholds. Then in the morning, when the town was plastered with eight inches of new snow, we realized the stranger at the door wasn't an axe murderer. It was Santa Claus.

I leaned into the front's interference scraping my goggles and skied. Weird temperature fluctuations distorted the snow pack. It was sticky, like Velcro, and you had to ski fast to scrape the frozen frizz off the top and get to the soft muff underneath. I crossed a road onto a steep wind scoured corner. The squishy powder suddenly thinned to bony patches. The ski edges bit on a bare spot and my feet spit ahead as they were smacked out from under me. The tilt of the mountain became acute and I was airborne, like Orion tilted in the winter sky. My arms swung wildly. In the bizarre light and with my goggles iced-up, I couldn't find the slope. I felt like I was hanging from a clothesline, one pin holding. I squeezed my pole grips as if they were the bars of a trapeze.

Just as I went limp, ready to fall, the wind sheared. My left ski found the hill. The right splashed down like the companion hull of a catamaran. Saved. But the skis settled on an island of exposed wind-polished ice. They accelerated and skidded sideways. Then they both whacked a soft berm. I was pitched again, in the opposite direction, airborne, horizonless and off keel. I was convinced I was going down. But, the wind flip-flopped. Switching from a stiff-arm mashing squarely in my chest, it figure-eighted around and pushed me from behind, cinching up under my arms. I vaulted upright, as if the same unseen hands dunking me the moment before had suddenly yanked me up. The skis came underneath me; my weight was miraculously centered. A glowing, interior rush melted the cloying pallor that engulfed me. I was giddy with relief. *I'm lucky. I'm lucky*, I thought. *I can walk under ladders.*

By the end of the run, my goggles were crackled with a kaleidoscope of ice. I scratched away two portals again. The feral turbulence of the blizzard had clawed deep drifts around every chairlift tower, every corner of every building, every stick of bamboo, every shaft of every sign, reminding me that five inches of whipsawed chaff was just the beginning. That wind shear that had plucked me from disaster told me that this storm was actually two storms slamming into each other. Monsoon moisture, warmish and muggy, funneled up from the Gulf of Mexico, 1,700 miles away, and rammed into a system carried out of the Pacific Northwest by the arctic jet stream. It meant critical mass, snow erupting from the collision.

Skiing run after run without a ticket, I felt like a little boy in a Rockwell print, outrunning a spanking with a stack of books jammed down my trousers. The storm intensified. Burrs of snow stuck to everything. Chair pads, lift towers, skis, ski poles, skiers. The folds of my parka, gloves, and bibs froze stiff as tin foil. The snow didn't so much fall as unscrew itself from the air. It seemed impossible that any of it reached the ground. I skied into a winding, white gullet. The taste of it turned labial, sweet. It was rooty— peat with a snip of fresh celery—and dusty, with the garden-sharp bite of radish and washed greens. There was a subtle neutralizing garnish, too...parsley. I scratched at my goggles constantly. The skis floated to the edges of trails, banked off rolls, snuggled near the trees, sliced along the shoulder of a trough (a snow covered creek). They lifted and dropped me over rows of grave-sized mounds, then shoved me over a traversing road. I had no blue print, no visualiza- tion of where I was going. It was a dance. I stood on the skis like a boy on his mother's toes and they found the rhythm, made the moves. I pressed my shoulders, hips, knees, and feet forward. My fists reached and gripped. The skis whiffed through white froth, curtains sprayed from their tips.

Time passed. The lift operator was covered in white chunder, freez- ing. She was shoveled-out, beat. It was late. I was the only skier left. Everyone else, either cold or exhausted or worried about the roads went home—quite sensibly. Empty chairs cycled by, ghostly. I went up again. At the top, I slid to boundary ropes along the Divide. I leaned against the howl like a wing walker. On a clear winter day, the overlook would have had a view of a jagged rhombus, the west- ern partition of the pass, the fortress front of Colorado wilderness. On a clear day, the near range of acute, scalene peaks stabbed at the sky like a stack of broken plates swept up against a blood-blue wall. The steep faces and shunts and shakes of fractured granite leaned on each other, gleaming. Some days, they appeared pewter: aprons and shins and thighs of discarded armor. The rock's gaps and avalanche chutes, chinked and flossed with snow, rose from the steep V of a descending glacial valley. It seemed a thousand years since I'd seen that range—and like a thousand years might pass before I'd see it again. The snow stung my face like gravel thrown up by a passing semi. The wind folded and whacked the bamboo fence line wildly. I stared into vitreous, white shadows—into a massive empty hold.

As I skied past a trail marker too blurry to read, I realized I was midway down a run called Treasure. Back when I was twenty-two, I once shushed this run, 1.2 miles in seventy seconds on a pair of seven foot skis that would be considered prehistoric now.[23] That was before the two trees. In the middle of that schuss, the skis turned to swizzle sticks, frantically flapping and twisting. For eye protection I wore my duct-taped John Denver wire rims; my eyes teared like a Standard poodle. I'd shed my coat in favor of more aerodynamic neoprene ski bibs and a tight turtleneck; the windchill was probably twenty below zero. When I crossed the "finish line," I nearly crashed into the lodge and through the plate glass windows. I was as brave and as dumb as Thor in those days, enjoying the spotlight of the universe.

In present tense, I promised myself I was skiing half that fast, though the needle of my internal speedometer wobbled. Was I skiing too fast? Not fast enough? In the miasma, it was hard to tell. My goggles were glazed. I was tired. A hard burn niggled into my quads. It would have been more effort to stop than to keep cranking turns, so I kept going—fast. From memory, I knew the hill panned left, then doglegged right, pouring out onto an expansive, snow swept pasture. When I got to the flats, I could relax.

At the instant I visualized that relief, I was airborne, spread-eagle and off-kilter. I didn't know which way was up or down.

23 If you're doing the math, that's an average speed of sixty. Top speed, I'm guessing, might have been in the mid-seventies.

My body braced in the air, terrified. Figuratively, I'd been tipped from the nest and had awakened falling—a bad dream. The instant was an eternity of breathless panic. How far would I fall? My feet slammed into something hard, as if I'd leapt a set of stairs and pounded onto a landing. I folded, shoulders to knees, ankles to arm pits. I spurted forward, my ass riding the tails of the skis as they sledded ahead. Then I was tossed again, spread eagle again, muscles stone-stiff again, keeling like a falling tree over a deep, dark hole. I strained to get my skis under me. I did, just in time to slam flat-footed on the far lip of the pit. My chin dunked between my knees. My arms slapped toward the ground. I bounced into the air again, knowing I was going to flip.

Slow motion: piked like a long jumper, I looked down into yet another hole, this one as big as a dumpster. Before I went all the way over, my skis slammed the ground again, like a gymnast banging on the spring board in front of a pommel vault. My neck snapped forward and my nose nearly touched my ski tips as I reached desperately and my head whipped between my hyper-extended legs. Fighting to keep the skis under me, and I wondered why the heels of my bindings didn't release. They should have. I wondered why my heels didn't pull out of my boots. They should have. I wondered why my legs didn't break. They should have. In a weird flash, I remembered that I had loaned my skis to a friend at the end of the previous season. In the excitement of the first day of skiing, and overwhelmed by the thrill of skiing for free, I'd neglected to readjust the tension of the bindings. I remembered this as my right hamstring popped like a sun-rotted bungee cord. The muscle kept tearing as my palms stretched for the ground.

Fast forward: I flipped. I landed sitting, legs out, the tails of both skis hammered into the snow. My leg was injured badly enough that I had to use both arms to pull my right ski out of the snow. I was stuck like a butterfly pinned to a bulletin board. I was completely alone on the mountainside, but I had the sense that someone had seen the whole thing and they were gone and they were laughing. I swore I heard laughing. The empty chairs of a nearby lift loomed in the snowy air, but I thought there must be someone up there, just out of sight, laughing. The laugh wanted to echo but the storm muffled it. I pinpointed the sound. I recognized that laugh.

It was me.

Vreni found me sprawled on the couch with an ice pack under my leg.

"So, I see you called in today," she said.

"Yeah. I heard this storm was going to be measured in feet."

"How was it?"

"You know. Just another day of *free* skiing." I smiled.

"I thought you quit doing that," she said.

I shrugged. "They weren't checking, so…."

"What's with the ice?"

"It's nothing. I just had a little trouble with some unanticipated flipping."

"Unanticipated flipping. Is that what you call instant karma?"

"Instant karma's a song," I said. "You pay in the next life." In the next twenty-four hours, my leg went stiff as a flag pole. The burning pain kept me awake at night. I got an ultrasound. There was a dark hole in the muscle, a blood clot the size of a fist. The medical bills ran into the hundreds of dollars—about the cost of a season pass to Wolf Creek. I missed seven weeks of skiing. It was several more weeks before I was able to venture beyond a beginner run.

Although I'd already paid the price, I wanted to make amends. For three years, I didn't do anything. Then one spring day—after I'd driven up Wolf Creek Pass, sat at another construction zone, and saw that the lift operators weren't checking tickets—I threw my skis over my shoulder and climbed to that spot where, on my last day of free skiing, I had edged up to the boundary ropes and leaned into the howl. Across the deep valley I saw a jagged rhombus of the pass's western partition. The acute, scalene peaks stabbed at the sky like a stack of broken plates swept up against a blood-blue wall. The steep faces and shunts and shakes of fractured blue granite leaned against each other, gleaming. Then the light shifted subtly and they appeared pewter-green: aprons and shins and thighs of discarded armor. The rock's gaps and avalanche chutes, chinked and flossed with snow, rose over the steep V of the descending glacial valley. It was exactly as I remembered it, as if I'd seen it everyday for a thousand years.

After I recovered my breath from the climb, I skied to the bottom and bought a lift ticket.

ELEVEN

OUTBACK, WEDNESDAY

The light was moon-faced. The chairlift rose through a hall of spruce loaded to their armpits with snow. The Inuit call it Qali, snow that collects on trees. Visibility was nebulous. Dense clouds dipped into the trees. I was escalated into the veil. Empty, broom-swept chairs climbed ahead of me. The seat bench bounced under me as the cable clamp lubbed over four rubber-lined wheels. The rocker arm of the lift tower shifted. The cable thrummed between my chair and the chair up ahead. The benches of descending chairs, not yet swept, clacked on their hinges as they clunked over rocker wheels. Cakes of snow broke from the corners of their seats, fell two stories and pocked the narrow slope. The tower vibrated. The mountain vibrated. The trees unswaddled cradles of snow. Sugar sacks lumped down on flour sacks which lumped down on potato sacks which lumped down on onion sacks which lumped down on cotton sacks, until, like futons tumbling from the sky, the foundered Qali found snowpack.

It was a Wednesday, I think.

Two college guys swung their twin tips impatiently on the chair behind me. Below them was a long bracelet of empty chairs climbing from the quiet gloom. At the top, I unloaded to the right and slid with viscous ease into the thick scrim. Snowcats had packed a road along the Divide. Three inches of nougat had collected since. Either side of the cat track, eight inches of new snow covered yesterday's powder. I gathered speed on the flat and skied into it. It had the slow second hand feel of a thick pelt. My tips cribbed under a wind-pressed top layer. Lower layers crumbled like a delicate pastry. Even deeper, the ski edges sunk to a grouty, old surface. Slopes rolled off the east side of the ridge into murky clouds. I swooped for a wide incline. The speed picked up. The descent was lumpy. The soft footload shifted unpredictably. The turns bucked or bottomed-out randomly. The skis punched through white mounds the size of stuff sacks and bean bag chairs, which exploded into confetti.

A few days later, Phil, a lanky, surefooted hiker, lover of mild-weathered mesas and magpie grasslands, asked me, "What is it with you and storms?"

My answer: "That's where the planet began, in the swirl, the cold swirl of the universe. When God said, "Let there be light," there was no sun yet; there was a snow storm. That's why he has white hair and a white beard; for most of Genesis the universe was 441 degrees below zero. He was frickin' freezing. There wasn't even hell for a hand warmer yet."

Phil frowned from the brow up and smiled from the eyes down.

"I know it sounds like I'm full of it," I said. "I think I sound like I'm full of it. But a good storm feels like a good handwoven poncho. It actually feels warm."

"Ah! Back to the womb," he said, his brow lifting.

"Exactly. That and the pure contrariness of it." Most people relish warmth, dry, peace, clear vision. In a blizzard you seek the opposite—cold, wet, wind, frenzy, blindness. I told Phil I'd skied days when 2,400 skiers and riders sat on the floor of the lodge and played cards while fifty ticket holders split up an entire mountain of fresh snow. Being up there, and out there, and in it, when everyone else is down there huddled and safe—that has something to do with it, too. I knew what Phil was asking. Why not just watch a storm from your kitchen window, while you're doing the dishes? I explain like this:

> Q: If the snow falls in the forest and no one is there to hear
> it fall, does it make a sound?
> A: Of course, it does.
> Q: But, if the snow falls in the forest and there is no one
> there to see it fall, does it matter?
> A: Of course, it does. The snow doesn't *need* us.

Still, I feel in my gut, that snow falling matters *more* if there is someone there to see it and hear it. To see creation, to watch it happen, matters. This is species-centric, I know. But I believe that consciousness matters. It matters exactly because at its root is the craving to observe creation, in whatever form: a litter of kittens, a blooming rose, a meteor shower, a hurricane, the Big Bang. The horticulturalist in a greenhouse who turns and finds a Day Dream or a Whisper in bloom, or the astronomer on a lonely mountaintop as the Leonids braid from the night sky like electrified cornrows, feels exactly what I feel in a snowstorm: like *everything* matters more; like WE matter more. It's not just that creation is on display. What is important is that someone is paying attention, watching, listening. In a snowstorm, I'm tasting and feeling it, too. To be human, attendance is required.

With Phil's question still on my mind, I came across an account of the creation of stars. The language was full of the language of snow storms: gas shells, mixed vapors, discrete clouds, dust-like glass, dust-like diamonds, condensation, accumulations, fogs, translucence, dust clots, dust ropes, dusty filaments. I was reminded that comets are snowballs. The writer called the formative swirlings of stars a "birth cloud." She reiterated that, in the beginning the universe was cold, cold dust—icy dust. I emailed Phil:

> With regard to our conversation on storms. Found this in Hannah Holmes *The Secret Life of Dust*: "[Space] dust is not well defined," says Steve Beckwith, an astronomer who studied space dust before becoming Director of the Space Telescope Institute, which decides where to point the Hubble....."We don't know the precise shape or composition of the grains," he says. "Is it little spheres? Is it strings? Plant-like things? A lot of it is *probably little snowflake like things.*" [My emphasis] Still think I'm full of it?

Like a storm, the cosmos is lathered and sinuous. Nebulae snap with lightning. Aneurysms of energy belch from the pucker of black holes. Meteor belts circle galaxies, latched to their paths like weather fronts to jet streams. Like storms, fast-rotating spiral galaxies pinwheel on the road map of the universe.

When a storm comes and goes without me, I missed something. I missed the action, the process. I'm not a genuine witness. Everything's done. On those brilliant, clear powder days, it's too easy to get caught up in the show. The snow is there as if it were some personal talisman handed to you to prove how lucky you are. There's inevitably a moment when you look back on a slope of deep snow and see your tracks. An artistic satisfaction rises. *Look what I did!* Admiring your own signature across a winter mountain, it's hard not to feel a tincture of ownership. In a full-on storm, this misconception is less likely. The calligraphy disappears almost as quickly as you descend. Your tracks fill in before you can find them again. Without an artistic trace to gloat over, it's easier to remain in the moment, easier to supplicate and quiet the ego. In the splay of snowflakes sharp as throwing stars, it's easier to focus and be subsumed in prescience. It's easier to be reminded that the origin of the mountain goes back to all that swirling, cold dust, and that the granite composing it is itself the offspring of heaven's earliest, coldest thunder and lightning—just like you. No one knows better than a skier amidst a storm that nothing is solid. Everything moves. Everything slides—beginning to end—downhill: personalities, civilizations, snow.

Phil e-mailed back:

You're the kind of guy that would surf in a hurricane.

I replied:

Tried that once. A buddy loaned me a board and took me out into Hurricane Hugo off the Delaware coast. Too bad I didn't know how to surf.

Wednesday.

I skied ten runs before I crossed another track, then headed for the trees.

On the headwall between two runs my Fatboys, a pair of wide skis made especially for deep snow, chopped at the wind-teased powder. Five or six steep turns funneled to a brief opening in the trees. Below, the spruce cluttered the slope like racks of jousting lances. The skiing was tight, like squeezing your grocery cart through a holiday crowd. Twice the trees narrowed to gaps slim as checkout lines. I scrunched to fit between. Big mitts of slapping snow hung from branches. I crossed a long flat to the base area. Around the lodge, a parka-clad squad armed with scoop shovels, snow blowers, and snowcats was digging out for the third time in less than a week. They prepared for more snow, tomorrow.

The storm was a slow one and it covered Colorado. Counterclockwise low pressure chewed along the New Mexico border as it crawled east. Counterclockwise—that's the direction water flows in a toilet. That's how the system looked on TV Tuesday night. The wide, white flush moved again and again across the entire screen, across the West. I'd watched the computer generated pattern recycle over and over, as if it were a memory that hadn't happened yet.

Close to midnight, I'd bundled up, and went out in it. Three inches had already accumulated. The snow fell through a band of streetlight at a gentle slant. I walked in the pearly dark, down a desolate valley road of bare cottonwoods, their bark plashed phosphorescently. I watched a quiet, fast river flow under a bridge. Honey colored with distant yard light, the current was wadded with white, as if straw had been shoveled into the river. At a streetlight beyond the bridge, ten deer moved quietly, stirred by the muezzin of geese on a dark pond. By the time I returned to my room, the snow was shin deep. I watched the storm scroll across the TV screen one more time as I fell asleep thinking, *Here it comes.*

Wednesday.

I saved Outback for last. The chair that leads to it, occasionally closed for high winds, is a long, exposed ride. The empty chairs ahead and behind swung back and forth like box kites. The wind weighed down my wide skis. I scooted to the sidebar and wrapped an arm around it, holding my glove over my face to avoid frostbite. I draped the other arm over the seatback and grabbed a stay.

Windload—the snowy blowout from trees and drifts gusting off the Continental Divide—settles in the lee of Outback Ridge. A broad, crowned band of accumulation builds much deeper than the snowfall itself. I wasn't the only skier who knew the conditions were prime, but the hike out the ridge was straight into the blow. Indeed, as I started out it felt like the backbone of the mountain twisted like a broken suspension bridge. My parka and bibs flapped angrily. I plowed short, slippery, mechanical steps. To stay upright, I poked around behind me with my poles. The pole baskets were sucked into soft, deep snow. Thanks to goggles, I was wide-eyed, but I couldn't see much. The height of the mountain was lost. I knew I was somewhere above eleven thousand feet, but I felt as though I were a spider stuck in a slippery white sink. Drifts hooded stunted pines along the crest. I shuffled as near as I could to their protection. Tiny ice shards and granite flecks peppered my helmet, drowning out the fiery hiss of the storm.

I only continued because I had the hike memorized. I could find Outback the way you find the light switches in your dark house. The slope begins as an open outfield that rolltops off the Divide. About halfway down, it organizes to an infield, then spills through dugout shadows between trees. Typically, conditions there are irregular—junky, scrap heap. The sun applies a glazy bake to the south-facing snow and it skis like a ramp of broken table lamps. Turns are about as fun as punching your bare fists into a barrel of Legos. Part adventurer, part hermit, part masochist, I come out here even when the snow is unskiable drop-forge covered with wind slag. Why? Because I'm an idiot. But on this Wednesday I knew the snow would be soft as a puppy's milk-bloated belly.

In a late spring storm last year, the access to Outback was closed from the leeward side, so I climbed in from a lower alley—a steeper, longer hike—straight into a rump of sandblasting wind. With my skis on my shoulder, I postholed just below the cornice-line of the ridge. Visibility was a tossed salad and a spaghetti of white dust devils. To see, I had to duck. I plodded for the saddle. The wind charged. Instead of pluming off the mane of the mountain, the strafe came at the same angle as the slope. I'd hiked high enough to ski, but the wind was so strong I couldn't steady my legs. I couldn't get my skis on. I stumbled and sank deep into the snow. Vertigo overcame me as the best clue to my way out, the hole of my last step, filled in beside me.

This wasn't Everest. Less than two hundred yards away there were trees that would direct me to safety. On a clear day, I was a two minute ski from a lodge the size of a small airport. People were down there eating french fries and pizza. But I remembered blizzard legends of Colorado farmers disoriented and lost in the yard between a prairie house and a barn. One succumbed not ten yards from his own front door thinking he was lost. Taking a cue from Hansel and Gretel, homesteaders solved this problem by rolling out a string of yarn between the house and the barn before a storm's onset. But this wind would flense a braid of yarn. If I walked the wrong way, into wilderness and deeper into the blizzard, there wouldn't be a track to follow by the time anyone realized I was missing.

I dug in and curled up, wrapping my arms around my skis and poles. I waited. There wasn't much else to do. It was a hasty hibernation. I felt the reach of wilderness, not because my location was remote, but because the storm had come and my whereabouts were abruptly a secret. The wilderness had come to me. I was submerged in it. Call it lunar solitude: when you know that no one else knows where you are and you're seeing something you know no one else is seeing. Instantly, you realize your smallness, realize that the world is huge and insurmountable. It's possible to fall in love with this seclusion, for it is in these accidental moments that you understand the joy and the pathos of human memory, that yours is the only one of its kind. I knew below me was an untracked slope, pure and immaculate, and I didn't want to miss it. But when the squall subsided—not too soon, but soon enough, I hoped—I'd hike back down the ridge before the next flared up. If I could find that dark island of trees, I could switchback my way through the woods to the bottom.

Then, I was giggling. I remembered a storm the previous spring. I'd brought my friend Ted to Outback. Ted, a short, gray-bearded, Jack Nicholson look-alike with the mannerisms of an itchy baseball pitcher, had been on the Junior Ski Patrol at Solitude, Utah back in 1962. Since then he had played ball for the Marines, taught Spanish, and raised six kids, but he hadn't skied much. Exactly fifteen years my senior (we have the same birthday), Ted had been like a surrogate uncle during my angst-ridden twenties. So, when he became gripped in the torpor of divorce and a long spell of unemployment, I wanted to help. My plan was simple: a day of skiing. Ted, driven by militant thrift, would resist. I anticipated this and bribed him with a free lift ticket and a twelve-pack of Milwaukee's Best.

He dug up a pair of garage sale Spyder stretch pants, a homemade goose down vest, a short-billed hunting beanie, and a pair of snowmobile goggles. His technique, a narrow, cool-daddy stance assisted by some stem-christie edge-chops, came back to him quickly. A day turned into two; two turned into three. Re-energized, he bought a pair of ski boots in a second-hand shop and tracked down ticket discounts through the local grocery store. In the middle of March, on my way to catch the biggest storm of the year (forty-plus inches in three days), I dropped by Ted's trailer to invite him to come along and give my Fatboys a try. I figured, if powder skiing didn't cheer him up nothing would.

He gulped down half a carafe of coffee in the car, and after a couple of tame runs in some lofty crude, he had the hang of the powder skis. I decided he deserved the soothing pet of deep, untracked snow. We skated and herring-boned up the highside of Outback. Clouds moved across the mountain like slow box cars spilling white, ferny dust. Between the axles, we could see the slope was untracked. "We're lucky, Ted," I said. "Just wait for an opening and ski beside my tracks." The turns had the slow predictable heave of a wet trampoline. The deep powder kicked up like feathered boas. Splashes reached my chin. I buried my mouth behind the collar of my parka so as to avoid choking. I hadn't been in snow that deep for years, and I couldn't wait for Ted to feel it. I wanted him to feel the wild, white undertow and the psychic cocoon of wide-eyed, amniotic awareness that cast the rest of the world in a distant, irrelevant light. It would take a little luck and a good run, but on the Fatboys I knew he could regrasp the intuitive art of powder skiing.

I romped down the slope all the way to the flats, and turned to watch. Low clouds swirled in. When the slope opened up, Ted didn't move. Too far to shout and the storm howling anyway, I waved my arms, but he wasn't looking. He seemed to have lost something on the ground. His poles were stuck in the snow beside him. His gloves were off and shoved under his armpits. It looked like he was riffling in his vest pockets. At first, I thought maybe he was fumbling for a stick of gum. I wondered if he'd lost his lift ticket. I worried that there was a problem with his bindings. My instinct was to help, but the climb up to him would have taken an hour in the deep snow, maybe more. It would be quicker to go back to the chair lift and skate back out the ridge. That would take around twenty minutes. If he was in serious trouble, I'd go to the bottom of the chair and phone the ski patrol shack at the top. But I didn't want to call out a rescue unless the situation were serious.

Another cloud passed over the slope. When it cleared, Ted reappeared in an odd, semi-balanced Kokopelli-like stance. Then I recognized what was happening. That half-carafe of coffee had kicked in. At the exposed apex of Outback in the heart of the biggest storm to hit the Sawatch Range in five years, fighting forty mile-an-hour gusts and a windchill of minus three, Ted had decided to pee. He seemed to be about half done when one of his gloves dropped to the snow. As the wind caught it, he instinctively made a stab at it with his free hand. The glove danced uphill. Desperate, he leaned uphill for it. The fat powder skis shuffled backwards. He looked like a man in two casts moon walking as a hundred dollar bill skittered away from him in a windy parking lot. I saw that he had not just dropped his fly but his vest and his pants were wide open. As he struggled to move forward, his pants slipped down his legs and he fell over. Half keeled in the deep snow, he groped for the glove with a ski pole. He loosened the chin strap on his beanie, which left him no free hand to reach for his lost glove.

From a distance, this was a black-and-white silent film with the same scratchy, snowy contrasts of Chaplin's *Gold Rush*. I remembered the scene when the luck-bitten tramp, immediately after a dinner of his own boot soles, is stuck in a cabin that has been pushed to the cliff-edge by an avalanche. The cabin teeters toward the precipice when Chaplin reaches for the door. He can't go out that way or the house will go over with him in it. But if he jumps out the window on the opposite wall, he'll be stranded without shelter in a deadly Alaskan blizzard. What to do?

The wind lifted and dropped Ted's glove again. Another gust might carry it off the other side of the pass. He paused, deciding. He reached for the other ski pole and worked himself upright. I saw what was coming next, and though I knew the storm would erase my words before they left my mouth, I screamed, "NO!" I watched in horror. Pants still opened and unzipped, he poked the tip of a pole into the lever on the heel piece of a binding. A boot came free. He took one step and three-quarters of his body sank into snow. He thrashed, the snow swallowing him like quicksand. There was only one way to help. I had to get on the chair and hike back out the ridge. He wasn't hurt. He wasn't injured. He was just stuck. It was cold, but he couldn't freeze to death in twenty minutes, so I didn't see the need to call the ski patrol. By the time I got back to the spot, he was gone. The storm was still thick and the wind was feral. For as far as I could see, the slope was an uninterrupted white field. There were no tracks. Any sign of struggle was blown in. I wondered if I'd come to the wrong spot or if Ted had choked and lay asphyxiated while an intense ground blizzard buried him.

I poked around with my ski poles until I was convinced he wasn't there. As I skied out, I saw traces of tracks lower down—mine from the previous run and a more erratic zigzagged set. The zigzags had to be Ted's. By the time I reached the chairlift, I convinced myself they were his. I checked the racks in front of the lodge. I didn't see the Fatboys, so I concluded that he was still out on the mountain, skiing, looking for me. I thought he might go straight back to the ridge.

I hiked and skied Outback five more times. My final run ended halfway down when I slammed a drift I never saw and tumbled. As I flipped into a comfy seat of powder, my right ski hurtled over me, landed below me on the soft slope ski-tip-up and bottom down, and planed over the snow straight down the hill. Unimpeded, it reached the flats two hundred yards away at about fifty miles per hour. It carved a looping left turn—exactly the arc I would have taken if I were on it—and disappeared around the bend. With only one ski to navigate a sea of bottomless snow, I felt very, very... alone. The long trek to retrieve my runaway was a combination of frothy, pogo-ing traverses and sloppy, amphibious crawling. In the midst of it, I wondered if Ted had sent out the ski patrol to look for me. When I finally did get back to the lodge, I found him in front of the fireplace, his wet gear littered across the seats of a cafeteria table. The wings of his bald head were scrambled as if he'd just arisen from a nightmare, or a baptism. He was grinning like a jack-in-the-box. "Wasn't! That! Great!" he said. He was crazy-assed loony with joy.

"I'll be right back," I said, striding for the stairs. "I gotta pee."

Two hundred and fifty million years ago, the Rockies were formed when granite punched up through a roof of seafloor sediments. Some thirty million years ago, they were covered under a pack of their own volcanic ash. The dust filed in Jackson Hole nineteen thousand feet deep. An expansive flat covered the mountains of Colorado, Wyoming, and Nebraska. A few of the highest peaks stuck out like baby teeth. Then, in the late Miocene epoch, maybe ten million years ago, the earth developed a case of the bloats, and everything pushed up another mile.

The existing plain, accustomed to the barely detectable pitch of an old mobile home, suddenly became an A-frame. John McPhee, author of the classic *Rising from the Plain* describes the action thus: "In response to the uplift, the easygoing streams that had aimlessly wandered the Miocene plain began to straighten, rush and cut, moving their boulders and gravels in the way that chain saws move their teeth." The advance and retreat of glacial ice caps accelerated the process, adding abrupt periods of melt and wet weather which created flash floods of immense power that lasted full seasons and were repeated decade after decade. McPhee describes the old rivers slashing at the land like barbed wire through skin, and then gnashing at the bones underneath. "After they worked their way down to the ranges, they sawed through them," he writes.

Eventually, enough crust was carried away that the granite underneath sprouted. Assisting the rage of advancing and receding ice was the wind. Its rotation and thrust grinded away at the subsummit deposition like belt sanders and Dremels. Expanding ice, salt, and lichen wedged into pink and blue granites. The rock popped open and crumbled, and a million years of wind turned the kernels to sand. What we call the Rockies is the muck of all this. What we think of as the spectacular ranges—the Cascades, the Tetons, the Sangre de Cristos, are really just a few bladed, needley, remnants of enamel surviving in the bottom row of a blue-mounded skull. Bad teeth still whistling in the wind.

When I hike Outback Ridge, I don't have to be reminded that half of the erosion that filed the Rockies down to their present nerve ends was from wind. It's the same wind that dropped tons of Colorado grime off the coast of Georgia in a two-day storm in the '70s, the same wind that suffocated babies in Prowers County,

Colorado in 1932, the same wind that steel-plated the Great Plains with ice in the Big Freeze of 1886—when you could walk from the Snowy Range in Wyoming to the Brazos river in Texas on the carcasses of dead cattle. Seventy-five miles from Outback, my house sat on the ancient lake bed of an Oligocene formation. At the east end of the valley tourists sort fossils from road cut limestone as if they were choosing from a rack of greeting cards. *Upwind*, at the west end of the valley even professional paleontologists have failed to locate one fossil.

Today's blizzards are fossils of that prevailing wind and harbingers of where we're all headed when we're finally dust. In a storm that lasts a day or two, the breath of the North American continent will blow us east, back where we came from—back to fill the features of the old land, maybe those low vulnerable Appalachians; or maybe we'll blow all the way to the Atlantic—our memories as significant as the swiggling lines of our existence, as meaningful and meaningless, as transitory and important as the footpaths of mites swept from a sunny window sill.

Wednesday.

The blasts of the front ripped out of the west, scouring the crease of Outback Ridge. The windward edge was scrubbed to pulverized, bare granite. Along the top, bristlecone were capped with drifts that reached over and scalloped a cat track that blazed the Divide like the walkway of the Great Wall. Every move forward was a step into the strike zone. Visibility was a little better at belt level, so I ducked under the gusts. I turned my head to avoid sucking up mouthfuls of sharp ash. My sinuses, already numb, knew what I was swallowing: ozone, sulfur, smectite, lichen fungi, pesticides, forest fire ash, diesel soot, lead, a little mercury, some strontium, the dandruff of Los Angelenos. I thought I tasted the tobacco smoke of my dying father's spit-ended cigars and the tang of sour cherries my mother picked from her backyard. Some of the ashes in the back of my throat didn't melt. They were sand. In the book on dust I'd read: "Magnified, an aging sand grain looks like an aging mountain: it is rounded on top but grooved with 'ravines' carved by tiny 'rivers.' And at the base of a 'cliff' is a sprinkling of 'talus,' fallen boulders one-hundredth of a hair wide." I made a note to e-mail Phil. *Mountains*, I'd tell him, *I breathe whole mountains.*

The hike felt far. On the last short hump, the wind was too much. Visibility was scrambled with flashes of whiteout. I took my skis off and carried them. I staggered past tracks to the left that scribble off the shoulder of the mountain down a soft, oft-skied glade. Tempting, but the crest of the saddle was just a short climb away. With each step, I tapped with my boot toes to make sure I found the crust of the cat track and didn't wander into soft, bottomless snow. Finally, I felt my heels under me. I dropped my skis on a solid spot, clipped in, pushed off. My balance compensating for the cross wind, I surfed upside of drifts, from scabby spots into meringue curls, dropping off and check-turning back at them. The drifty cat track swaled down into calmer air. Blown snow arched over me and fell like a mist. The expanse of Outback was below. I pivoted hard on my right ski. It responded like a spring, propelling me across and launching me off the skiddy road. There was Outback, under me, an untouched, white dome, swollen with a sea of pure, new snow, cosseted by the feathery heavens.

The kinesiology of the short flight lobbed me, like a ball swishing into a net. It's worth pausing to describe this. The flying/falling sensation is almost identical to that of a first kiss. Where one will land can't be exactly predicted. Aim is not so much the concern as commitment and faith. You lead with open hands, feeling for the hips and pitch of your descent. Your strong foot also leads; it, and not the kiss, is what will eventually catch you.[24] For balance your head tilts against the direction of your inertia, like leaning into a fast turn when driving a car. If you're doing it right, a brief moment feels like eternity; you'll lose the feeling of your feet and hands; you may lose an awareness of the middle of your body; you may become conscious of a floating, swirling, concentric spinning somewhere between your hips and your belly button, as if your ass simply fell out on the ground behind you—in the snow, right next to your steaming heart. As gravity pulls you in, the world becomes limpid, warm, soft, windless. You are suddenly adrift in the gleam of another's eyes. Your nose—even if it were clogged with lichen fungi the moment before—will find an ocean side of oxygen; your teeth will loosen; your lips will tingle. Descend. Wrap your hands around just so. You'll feel like you're giving your life away, like universes are being created. Of course, you are, and they are, because from the moment of that first kiss, you'll want one thing above all else and one thing only: More.[25]

I didn't stop in the flats. I tucked downhiller-style, hopped the chair again, trekked the ridge, and launched onto Outback from that same crusty, drifty, barely visible cat track. For two runs, I lunged to the right of my first tracks. For two more, I check-marked to the left. On the sixth hike, three nodding skier-shadows shuffled out the ridge ahead of me. Their distant figures disappeared as I caught up. I snapped into my skis, hurried. More shadows appeared back in the milky air. They came like cows through a dropped gate. By the time I herringboned to the crest, the skiers ahead of me had emptied off the slope. Their tracks weaved away, down into the basement of the storm.

24 If you aren't sure which your strong foot is, or haven't had your first kiss yet: put your feet together; close your eyes; and have someone push you from behind. That's it.
25 I'm convinced that when skiers say that skiing is better than sex, this is precisely what they mean but can only partly articulate. What they mean is: This is better than sex; it's as good as a dump truck full of first kisses.

TWELVE

ANOTHER STORM

There are no secrets anymore. When a slow winter system out of the northwest humps six feet of snow on the Wasatch, keeps moving and drops thirty more in Colorado, everybody knows it. In the old days a few locals would show up. Then came the Weather Channel and the Internet. Every junkie within five hundred miles knows exactly where it's snowing and how much. They study satellite images, spot storm trajectories, set alarms, sleep in long underwear and goggles and drive for dark hours on winding, icy roads. A ski bum waiting to ski deep, untouched snow is like a day trader waiting for the announcement of a sexy new IPO. It's a scrum to get your share. Lifts open at nine sharp. I'm always late. I'm ashamed I'm not up there, first. I used to be first. Now, my wipers slap at gravel spitting from a snow plow's rear end. Vreni grips her seat and armrest as I repeatedly nudge out into the opposite lane, but I can't see to get around. I crawl up passes at twenty miles per hour pouting.

By 8:40, I was buckling my boots, but squads of skiers and boarders were already nosed up to the lift line. I got panicky, possessive, jealous. By the time I got out there, a white-haired lift operator in moon boots herded everyone back beyond a maze of bamboo and rope. The pack was fighting mad and ecstatic. The colors of parkas—bumblebee yellow, basketball orange, lichen green—oscillated like electrons and protons passing in a compressing orbit. There were sixty of us, and more coming. A stream of cars filled the parking lot. Above and behind us, eight hundred vertical feet of breasty, virgin slopes awaited.

It's likely that everyone knew the chair we were egging to get on had been closed for three days due to high winds and low visibility. We all believed we were about to get lucky. We already were lucky. It was still snowing, hard. A steady blaze of bleached asterisks fanned from a sky of pixeled luminescence. White clouds slipped down the mountainsides. Adding to the arousal was the fact that this was the first big storm of the season. November and December barely coughed on the Rockies. Thus far, the snow had come in teases of fern-like bikini muff—sugary frostwork, an inch or half-inch at a time, nothing like the lusty deep powder skiers wantonly craved and *needed*.

At 8:55 a.m., I slid my fat skis forward with everyone else. The slippery mob crunched into one throbbing muscle. "Let's gOhO-hOhOh," someone mooed. "Hup! Hup!" another hooted. I looked back, up the mountain, into the squall. The snow fell as steadily as the sand in an hour glass. A lift operator—half a wastebasket of shredded paper for his beard—pushed a flatulent snow blower toward us, clearing a narrow canal in the deep snow. The blower vomited snow like exploding packs of freeze-dried saltines.

I rested my armpits on the handles of my ski poles and let my hands dangle. My gloves slapped to kill nervous energy. To my left, a slumped-back snowboard punk in an orange balaclava and silver goggles with Jolly Roger holograms seemed suspicious of my faded parka and my vintage powder skis.

"Holy cow, Dude," he moaned, looking down. "How wide *are* those?"

I smiled. He was right. They looked like old water skis, six foot tongue depressors. I said, "One hundred and thirty-four millimeters, wide, Dude—each. How wide is that little thing you got there?"

He looked down at his rental board. "Um, what's a millimeter?"

Poor kid. By eleven he'd be in the lodge playing Uno with his Young Life chaperone.

The snowblower gouged out just enough room for everyone to file in two-by-two. I estimated I'd end up in about the fifteenth chair. Thirty people would get to the top before I did, but that was okay. Most of them were snowboarders. They'd still be sitting to the side finishing their Winstons and ratcheting their bindings by the time I skated by them. There were a few respectable three-pinners ahead of me, but I figured the real sprint would come from a fistful of fast and furious straight-liners. That was fine. Those guys would schuss thirty inches of virgin powder. Great. Straight tracks leave plenty for me. At 9:00, the herd stampeded. Elbows were thrown. Skis and snowboards stomped aggressively. A few indignant oaths yipped over the melee, but lift line protocol prevailed once we were in the confines of bamboo and rope and we all soon swung in the wintry sky.

The mountain top was wind scoured, but on the slope, snow piled up to my ankles, then my knees. I traversed, scouting an expert run that tipped from the heights like a dentist's chair. The straight-liners were already throwing up dusty contrails as they drag raced right down the middle. My skis spermed, left to the flanks of a moderate, wide run. The wind drove snow like soapy shower curtains. Swirling ground blizzards crosscutted snow drifts stretching out onto the slope. Half an inch of frosty fur topped twenty-nine-and-a-half inches of soft belly. Except for breathing and the susurration of snow passing—deep as my hips now—I traveled in silence. The easy rhythm of the turns was waltzy. You could ski snow like this on a couple of seesaw planks, or ride it on a raft of sheet rock.

I looked into trees on my right and aimed at a white flash between two tall pines, a slit the width of a turnstile leaked to steeper and, I hoped, deeper pitches. The skis prowed, bogged for bottom as I steered them through. My weight sank with them. My arches gripped. Snow burst up in front of me. The ski's tips surfaced, like dolphins and dived like dolphins into the clear of a bright, descending alley, steep as stairs. The skis lofted, banked, and bucketed. Blocked from the wind, the snow was chiffon. It swished as high as my chest. I was tossed out by a drift and thrown into another. I swatted snow-loaded branches. The glade got roomy, and the skis spooned in and out of the spunky snow. My knees and hips dropped low. My chest crunched forward, for speed, but the trees tightened. I had to pull back. The snow dragged magnetically. I angled hard to duck branches. The blizzard shadows became boreal. I popped from the forest onto an open flat. Out of the cover I leaned against a blasting wind. My skis found a track. I looked back up the mountain. The run above, the one those straight-liners got to, was plunked with potholes, lashed with zigzags. A Telemarker squirmed in the snow near the top, poles and skis thrashing like the legs of a drowning bug. An overturned snowboarder rocked in the sauce, like a turtle flipped on its shell.

Vreni was waiting at the lift line, her silver helmet screwed tightly to the collar of her parka. On the chair we ascended into the white heavens. It was cold. We hardly spoke. At the top, she needed no advice from me. She had her own fat skis and she was off to her own caches while I floored it back to my glade. I let the skis loose and hung on. I wanted to ski exactly the same run, relive it if I could. I was tempted to jump into the old trench and ride it, but that wasn't possible. I've tried. You get going too fast. To make those loopy, bulging turns, you need the resistance of the deep snow. Its embrace is crucial to the floating rhythm. It can never be the same. Even on a fresh day. The temperature is different. The snow is different. The light is different. It might be delightful, joyous—even orgasmic—but never the same. It makes skiing as sad as jazz. All improvised and all lost in the midst of its own becoming. Every moment hangs in memory, the phenomenology forever internal and terminal. When the memory goes, it's gone. You can never go back—not exactly.

I made rounder, deeper turns this time, leering near the old tracks. A new turn bloated over the lip of an old one. I veered sharply to avoid the collapse, darting into the crowded timber. Symmetrical hairpins became quick skips. Trees closed in. I battled off arm tackles of spruce. The skis reined to a halt. The snow, animated and viscous the instant before, caved. I was captured thigh-deep in a cold lump. My quads burned, stony with pain. My goggles fogged. My helmet steamed. I gasped in afterglow. In my powder lust, I'd forgotten to breathe. I looked back. My last umbilical tracks climbed into the open glow of the glade above.

I didn't have to wait long for Vreni. Her fat boards galloped along the chundered flats with supple skill. Her parka and bibs were slabbed with snow. She was smiling, every tooth as white as the shameless, decadent white of the storm. She cuffed a long turn and stopped. Her goggles were fogged. Her helmet was glazed and steaming. "You forgot to breathe, didn't you?" I asked.

"These are great skis!" she said, breathless. Hers had the same pizzazz-less tongue depressor shape as mine but were shorter. I bought them for her in a thrift shop one Valentine's Day. They were old Rossignols. In French, Rossignol means *nightingale*. *My nightingale*, I thought, as she smiled. A tattered rental label still clung to the skis. It read: "PROPERTY OF HEAVENLY." *Yes. Heavenly*, I thought. *The storm. The snow. This day. Her.*

"Second best Valentine's gift I ever bought," I said.

"What was the best?" she asked.

"A pair of red stretch pants I bought an old girlfriend."

"Who was that?"

"Some chick I knew back when I was a ski bum." We piled onto the chair, besotted, radiating. Swinging up in the blazing whiteness, we heard an orgy of whoops and yawps from the woods. My glade discovered. Alas. We moved to a lift higher up. The blizzard washed over the mountain top as we unloaded. We tilted against the splintery wind, feeling our way along a ridge. I slalomed around side-hill trees that collared creamy snow over a crest. The fat skis floated. I garlanded up onto a steep sidewall. The slope below was tumescent and milk-white, dropping into blanched shadows. My body punched through thick fleece. Loosened snow cascaded over my arms as I blew through it. The skis dropped away, hanging and then bucking as they caught me. My boots kicked up almost to my arm pits. Turns vaulted under the surface of the snow. My head floated near the surface. Even when I hopped a buried boulder, a white mass swirled. Billowing, white hunks flew, sailing with me into a turn that dunked chest-deep.

This was exactly what I hoped to find—an eight second ride. The white buffalo between my legs stomped and jumped. I held on, chin tucked, weightless between the bounds. In that instant of suspension, sweet oblivion quivered under my feet and delight banged my ribs like the bassist in a funk band.

At the lift, I discovered that Vreni had been playing around behind my back. She'd hopped over the ridge beyond cliff glades to a little single-wide, hose-bend of a slope called Dire Straits.

"A-where d'ya think ya going?" I said.

She told me I was crazy, and she said, "Hey, baby. I'm your wife."

I said, "You know I like you to be free."

She told me I was crazy, gambling with my life.

I said, "I think you better go with me girl."

But she didn't. Off the chair, she was gone to Dire Straits again.

I stuck to my guns for another run of face-shots. One more time that steep shoulder was all mine. I plummeted. Snow splashed like pipe cleaners around my collar. I circled the boulder. My weight across the mushroom that capped it marled the snow off. As I curled under, I was broadsided by a white wall, swallowed. I inverted, cart-wheeled. Sweet, weightless oblivion and white light enveloped me, no up or down. Snow swiped across my goggles like socks in a Laundromat dryer. Whumph! I landed on my butt buried in a white mound soft as shredded coconut. One ski was in my lap like a TV tray. The other protruded from the snow close by, like a spear in the side of a wooly mammoth. Flushed and giggling, I dug out of the swimmy froth.

Vreni was waiting. "Where ya been?" she said.

I shrugged. "Even a hero takes a bullet in the chest."

"Yeah," she said. "I thought you fell."

THIRTEEN

DOCUMENTATION: THE WORLD SAND
SPEED SKIING CHAMPIONSHIPS, JULY 29, 2005

Colorado's southern most alpine valley is bigger than Connecticut. And it's not what you're picturing. It's flat desert. The soil is salty with bunches of trashy, tangled shrubs—rabbitbrush, saltbush, sage. Several dwarfed versions of cactus turn up in the pale, dry dirt. (Vreni calls it "unattractive dirt.") Theoretically, they flower. I've seen photos of Starvation Prickly Pear with a yellow, rose-like bloom. There's plenty of yucca, and, where the acidity isn't too high, scatters of tough, perpetually grey grasses. This—fifty miles wide and a hundred miles long, down to New Mexico. East: the fortress walls of the Sangre de Cristo Range. West: the massive resurgent domes of the San Juans. Paul Simon mentioned the Sangres in his song "Hearts and Bones." The lyric goes: *Traveling together/In the Sangre de Christos....* It's melancholy, about separation, loss, dissonance. I have to believe the title had O'Keefe in mind, but he claims it came from Yeats. (I've always thought of it as west-of-the-Mississippi version of his song "Graceland.") I guess he didn't look at the map when he spelled *Cristo*. Alpine means the entire valley floor is above seven thousand feet. It's cold most of the year, below zero every winter night. It's a dry cold—freeze-dried, dry-ice cold. It rarely cracks eighty in the summer.

Shallow wetlands interrupt the arid flats. They attract geese, pelicans, and avocets. Thanks to the highest concentration of pivot sprinklers in the world, disc-shaped fields of potatoes, alfalfa, barley, lettuce, and canola checker the valley floor. Thousands of Sandhill cranes can't resist. They flock to grain fields and stay for weeks in fall and spring as they migrate from Mexico to Canada and back.

Headed east, I aimed our '92 Buick Roadmaster station wagon at a low notch in the Sangres, a distant pass. It's kick-back driving. Seven Mile Road, a chip-seal affair of tars and gravels rolled together like squashed bran muffins, is a gunbarrel for thirty miles. The car's faux-wood sides peeled. The drooping headliner fluttered. The radio was missing a knob. There were other concerns: bad motor mounts, coolant leaks, juking ball joints. The anti-lock brakes only worked on the right side. The air conditioner was shot. Airbag, too. The driver's side window disappeared into the door like a dagger board and wouldn't come out. The heater fan stuck, but only when it got cold. The left turn signal and driver's side power seat still worked, and when you flattened the back there was room for twenty-five sheets of plywood. Duct-taped to the back window, a sheet of custom cut visquine flapped a lot. I eyed the oil pressure and the temperature gauge.

Vreni wore sunglasses and some sort of gardening hat. She concentrated on the sky. It kept her mind off hundreds of square miles of "unattractive dirt." I'd say she was sitting beside me, but actually she was about three feet away, opposite a very generous armrest/console/cup holder that split the bench seat. I drank Coca-Cola, made with sugar, from a glass bottle—"refresco," "retornable," "Hecho en Mexico." We'd packed a cooler, camp seats, groceries in paper bags, Styrofoam plates, plastic wear, paper towels, Off, and sun block. The tips of my 180 centimeter Atomic Fatboys jutted

out the flapping back. A radio station out of Red River/Questa—
the station out of Red River/Questa—played a morning of B sides.
The Roadmaster had Quad.

"That's what I like," Vreni said. "Jethro Tull first thing in the
morning,"

"Yeah. Makes me want to run down to the pancake house and
smoke a cigarette."

"I wasn't thinking of that!"

"Then you're missing the essence of Tull in the morning. Did I
bring the cordless drill and the water skis?"

"Yes."

"Good."

"What's the drill for?"

"You'll see."

On a straight run, it's five stop signs (you only need to stop at
three) and a jog over to the Six Mile to get to the Great Sand Dunes
National Park and Preserve, a.k.a. Great Sand Dunes National
Monument. But we had to stop by Pat's and Page's on the way.
He's got a four acre corner, featuring a clapboard two-story, leaning post-and-beam barn, a concrete silo about forty feet high, some
pipe fenced corrals, and a couple of small steel silos beside a circle
of alfalfa. As we pulled up, he was ferrying picnic gear plus a baby
stroller, gas grill, rock skis, two pairs of near-vintage Nordica ski
boots, bent ski poles, and a mid-sized backpack through a chain-
link gate, piling it all beside his new dual cab 4X4 pickup. He's tall,
with the chlorine-blue eyes, sharp shoulders, and the close-cropped
head of a competitive swimmer. Pat and I skied together, mostly at
a small, cold area in the high Sawatch Range. He was outstanding
in the bumps and powder, and good with gadgets—camcorders,
GPS systems, computers, etc. He also liked to hike for his turns.
Page, his wife, was watering flowers. She was a rosy-faced, golden-

haired, Norse ski goddess—willing to ski in bitter cold, and willing to watch Katherine, their spunky two-year-old, while Pat got in a few runs. Katherine, with pelican blonde hair, chlorine-blue eyes and Norse features of her own, wrapped her long fingers around my pinky before I was even out of the car. She dragged me to the corrals. We petted the yellow rump of an Appaloosa colt, soft as down. Katherine yelped with glee. She dragged me back to the house, plopped onto her diaper, laid her face flat on the sidewalk and sucked from a stream of hose water. "Do you think she's thirsty?" I asked. Pat laughed.

"Do you think it will rain?" Page asked.

"Yes," Vreni said.

"Do you think it will be sunny?" Page asked.

"Yes," Vreni said.

"Should we bring the grill?" Pat asked.

"Sure," I said.

"Do you guys have mustard?"

"We have jalapeño mustard."

"Do you guys like barbeque sauce?"

"Does it have corn syrup?"

"Do you guys like sausage?"

"Love it."

"Should we bring chips?"

"We have vinegar and salt Pringles, sweet potato chips, tortilla chips, two bags of ruffled chips, cheese puffs, two six-packs of non-alcoholic beer, four Negro Modelos, four Sprites—in bottles—and four Coca-Colas—in bottles."

"In bottles. Impressive."

"I mean *glass* bottles."

"Oh, *glass*." Pat was impressed. "Where did you find those?"

"Jack's in Del Norte. Heche en Mexico."

"That's hecho," Page said.

"Oh yeah, hecho."

"Do those have corn syrup?"

"The ingredients say 'high fructose corn syrup *and/or* sugar.'"

"So you're gambling."

"I'm gambling."

"We were thinking we'd run to the hardware and get some rocks for the grill," Pat said. "These are pretty dirty."

I looked at the rocks. "They're okay. Let's go."

"You think so?"

"How dirty can they be," I shrugged. "They're rocks. Let's go."

"That might be corn syrup crusted on there," Pat warned.

"I think once it turns to carbon, the proteins are burned off."

Finally, we headed out. Pat pulled up beside me at the end of the driveway. "Do we have everything?"

"Yes," I said. "I have the cordless drill."

He laughed. "It's always good to have one of those on a picnic."

He followed me down the road, but at a distance.

"Maybe he's afraid the Fatboys will fall out," I said.

"Maybe you're doing seventy in a fifty-five," Vreni said.

"I never saw a sign," I said.

"They don't have signs on roads like these."

Telephone wires sagged from poles with no cross-pieces. Sheep fence topped with barbed wire sagged on bone-grey fence posts. Tumbleweeds stuck to them. In the brown corners of round green fields, stacks of hay twice as high as double-wides settled beside solitary bungalows. (In the old days you could buy the complete house kit from Sears). Poplars and cottonwoods were planted to the west as windbreaks. Every mile or so there was a potato cellar, either steel-framed or Quonset, large enough to cover a 747. They dwarfed old Gambrel barns with widows' peaks and vented cupolas. We passed a small high school, protruding from the desert floor like a mausoleum. The Masonic mix of blond and russet brick matched a cell-block elementary across the street. Behind it, a football field and track were flooded up to the curbs. We passed squatty galvanized silos, COOP logos fading, crossed railroad tracks—a local line less than ten miles long running north to south.

The enormous round fields changed color, toasty yellows alternating with verdant discs speckled with white and purple blooms. Throngs of sunflowers filled dusty, wide corners and the banks of irrigation ditches. A sprinkler spanned from the center of every field, like the girded, translucent wing of some Jurassic dragonfly. Toward the middle of the valley, into a land of littler rain and yanked water rights, we passed old single-wides aside drooping barns of unchinked logs and shakes.

At the highway, Pat went right for gas in Mosca. I told him to go on ahead and save us a spot. Vreni and I went left. The highway was a smoother, firmer chip-seal. It had a centerline and four inches of shoulder. "I read somewhere that most of the coal in the U.S. goes to China, so every time I see one of those endless trains of coal I think of China..." I rambled. Vreni smiled. She couldn't hear me over the wind of the open windows, KRDR blasting and the plastic whipping. "...When I see a gravel pit, I think of driving in Colorado." Before chip-seal, the Pueblo used the road, as early as 1300 A.D. The Athabaskan and Shoshonean used it before that. The Navajos told the Pueblos the Spanish were coming. That was five hundred years ago. The Navajos said the Spanish rode "from one place to another on animals that looked like large dogs." The conquistadors called the Navajos and Pueblos *caminates*. A *caminate* is "one who walks upon his land." It was a dis, a cut down. Wars were fought for control of the *Rio Bravo del Norte* (the Rio Grande). Now, a cooperative of ten federal, state, and regional agencies (plus the Nature Conservancy) calls the road *Los Caminos Antiguos*. It's hoped tourists will stop somewhere along the vacuous seventy mile gunbarrel. An interpretive marker—two decoupage panels stabbed into a gravel pull-out—was posted a hundred yards off the highway. The sign shrank in the foreground of the Sangre Range, like a miniscule footnote beneath a sky big enough to cover Connecticut.

"I bet you could get an acre out here for nothing?" I said.

"Are you kidding?" Vreni said.

"It's quiet."

"It's quiet at our house."

I tried to wipe the dirt off the sign. The surface felt like unevenly dried glue. "Is this varnish sun baked, or did they mean it to be that brown?"

"It sure is dark," Vreni said. "You can hardly read it."

"It looks like it was glazed with...corn syrup."

Random vehicles sped by back on the highway. Half were tractor-trailers. The most successful enterprise on the *Los Caminos Antiguos* is an Alligator Farm outside Hooper. Between three and four hundred alligators are sequestered in ponds fed by geothermally heated wells. The warm water allows cultivation of Tilapia—a staple of Denver's Vietnamese community. The gator farm is also a zoo for abandoned exotic pets—emus, pacu, parrots, pythons, rattlesnakes, tortoises, iguanas. Gator wrestling lessons are available. Succeed in wrestling a gator and you get an "Official Certificate of Insanity," and a photo of yourself saddled on a gator clutching its jaws with your bare hands. (Fail and you get an "Official Certificate of Stupidity," and an 8x10 of you with no hands.) Experts say, "Alligator wrestling is a lot like life itself. If you know what you want, don't hesitate and don't let go, for he who hesitates gets bit." It's claimed that anyone can wrestle a gator if he can overcome his mental fears. After an invigorating match with a man-eating reptile, you can visit the UFO Watchtower, just minutes down the road, set up at a point where "two vortexes radiate energy that has been said to heal the soul." The raised iron deck affords views of hundreds of square miles of unattractive dirt and two lonely mountain ranges.

The gas station in Hooper, one of three in seventy miles, has two pumps and an abandoned truck scale. A few flatbeds and dusty pick-ups were parked outside the adjoining café—"For Sale By Owner." Across the highway a tiny post office looked like it was once a gas sta-tion, too—flat roof with blue tin fascia shading peeled grey stucco. A carport clad in yellowing corrugated fiberglass attached to one side, a gutted phone booth to the other. The rest of town was behind the café. Two blocks wide and six blocks long, Hooper is a mosaic of defeat: screw-rusted single-wides; unpainted railroad shacks with four sided roofs and lean-to bathrooms and kitchens; an adobe or two; boarded storefronts; plank-sided sheds and tippy outhouses. Empty lots were stacked with rusty junk and gangled brush. Half the streets are pulverized dust, the other half were chip-seal. The heart of town was strewn with stunted, thickly branched cottonwoods that ignored property lines. At the south end of town a two-story brick See-Spot-Run elementary school and a large steel building (the gym and the cafeteria) were surrounded by a sea of green grass. The school's elaborate playground trumped the Town Park, a few blocks north, which consisted of the arches of half buried tractor tires, a swing set, some grass, and a sandy, weed-stippled softball field. Next to the park a church, with two long wings painted Amish-white, fit in a street corner. The steeple had an old fashion lightning rod. A concrete handicap ramp ascended the entrance beside beds of neatly arranged purple, yellow, and red flowers. The edge of town sported a small dirt-bound development of half a dozen newer manufactured homes (half of them single-wides), and a U-Lock-It storage unit whose metal doors matched the post office. I cruised slowly to avoid dust getting sucked in the back window.

"I don't know why you won't live in Hooper," I said to Vreni.

"Because it's in the middle of nowhere and there's nothing here and there's no one here."

"There used to be a car dealer here."

"In 1960?"

"I think they sold Model As."

There were three other towns on the *Los Caminos Antigua* almost exactly like Hooper—Mosca, Moffat, Villa Grove—evacuated, peaceful places under wistful, sun-washed skies with views of Teton-like peaks.

"I bet you could buy the biggest house in town for thirty-nine thousand," I said.

"You can live here," Vreni said, cheerfully. "Just not with me."

"Nobody would bother you here. Did you know that between 1910 and 1940 more livestock was shipped on the narrow gauge at Moffat than from any rail station in the country? That's just up the road."

"I'm not going to live there either."

"They drove sheep to La Garita and then all the way up to Snow Mesa above Creede. In the fall, they brought them all the way back. That's got to be a two hundred mile trip. Can you imagine a summer up on Snow Mesa? Twelve thousand feet, just you and the sheep, no one to bother you."

"With a bunch of sheep? No."

"How about without sheep?"

"No."

"You could see the herds coming to the railhead from miles away by the dust they kicked up. The herds surrounded the town for miles around as they waited to load up."

"And now there's no railroad at all, right?"

"The railroad shut down in '69. Did you know that the population and relative prosperity of thirty of Colorado's sixty-three counties peaked before World War II?"

"Why do you want to *live* in these places?"

"Just planning ahead," I said. Thinking about retirement. When we're through being cool and face the fact that we're squares, we'll have to decide where to park the RV."

"What RV?"

Ted and Jacob lived in a beige, vinyl-sided 14'X40' Nova mobile home skirted with hay bales. The back faced the dirt street. They bought the place from the guy who owns the gator farm. Vreni waited in the car. She'd never liked like the smell of ferret pee. In the yard, a pile of hay bales covered by old carpet circled the trunk of a cottonwood, a container of Gojo hand cleaner on top. By the trailer, a rusty flagpole was topped by a Christmas tree TV antenna. Excess wire hung in loops near the base. Ted's official bio, as reported by the *Colorado Gator Gazette*, reads: "Ted Lay moved his family to the San Luis Valley in 1978 to raise his kids 'where you can get your feet in the dirt.' He taught Spanish, English, and social studies for ten years and now provides Erwin and the fish operation with friendship and care. Ted appreciates the diversity of the valley, comparing the Sand Dunes with the Sahara and the Gator Farm with the Congo...." My favorite story about Ted is how he got two infield hits off Tom Seaver when the Marines played USC into extra innings. During Vietnam, Ted played for the Marine's recruiting team as utility outfielder and pinch-runner. At five-foot-six, with the jump of a cheetah, and running from the left side of the plate, he beat out the throws to first.

"You're early," He complained through the cracked louvers of the kitchen window.

"It's ten-fifteen, man."

A folding table was erected by the gate of a low board fence. Underneath it, empty jugs of motor oil were strewn beside a small stack of bricks. The boards connected to wire fence and then back to taller boards at the boundary of the dirt lot. Bushes grew through the wire sections. Extension cords and hoses crisscrossed the weedy yard. There were plenty of shady trees around, filled with raucous birds. I heard a chicken. In a far corner of the yard a doorway followed a sloping roof line down to a subterranean structure, a well house. In the opposite corner, along an alley, a dilapidated storage shed with a basketball goal that lay flat on the roof was surrounded by spilling piles of old boards and plywood. A roll of snow fence leaned on a clothesline post not far from a weight bench. A few steps from the shed, an outhouse with a refrigerator leaning against it backed up to another tall pile of boards. A state-of-the-art satellite dish was bolted to a telephone pole in the middle of the yard. Another telephone pole, between the outhouse and the shed, had a second refrigerator chained and padlocked to it. In front of it, a wire bin was stuffed with sticks and dead branches.

Full sections of old carpet were spread over large areas of the yard, to kill weeds. It worked. Nearby there were areas of bald dirt. A girl's Columbia one-speed with rusty fenders and rotten whitewalls (a "Help American P.O.W.s" sticker on the chain guard) was parked by the steps to the back deck. A square of half-inch plywood covered a hole outside the back door. A fading cut of orange carpet fit into the far corner of the deck, where two blue bathroom mats hung on a shaky rail over a five gallon wet/dry Shop-Vac and two empty cans of bulk chili beans. An upholstered easy chair, covered with carpet and plastic, bumped up against the house. A small Weber grill and a half-empty fifteen pound bag of Kingsford charcoal sat beside it. On the other side of the chair was a battered, rusty filing cabinet on wheels. Catty corner to that, a side-loading wood stove was shoved against the rails and draped with the covering torn off a bundle of insulation.

Next to the bathmats stood a sparkling, deluxe Uniflame barbeque smoker/grill. Airbrushed cobalt black, it shone as if it had been Turtle-waxed. The lid and bottom were elaborately vented, complimenting a plethora of varnished wooden handles and a large ash pot.

Ted met me in the dark doorway. He was shirtless. Though fit—he still runs wind sprints twice a week—he was a little too hairy (think Burt Reynolds), a little too gray, and little too bald to get away with it. Inside, the windows were cloaked with flannel blankets and ponchos. Dark paneling and brown carpet muted what light penetrated the open doorway. The ghostly glow of the TV and a musty, wet-hay, urine odor dominated the decor.

"Nice smoker. Got any smoked alligator legs?" I said.

"Yeah, well. That's Jacob's," Ted said.

"You know, winter—when it's cold—those wood stoves come in really handy. You can move them inside and put a chimney on them and burn wood."

"Happy birthday to you, too." Ted said, in a brotherly tone—generally vituperative while specifically affectionate.

"Happy birthday." I said. We hugged.

I met Ted when he was forty-five. We worked for minimum wage taking turns running a jackhammer and applying crack sealer to a crumbling chip-sealed parking lot. He invited me to his home for dinner with his wife and their six kids. The eight of them fit in a soft-bricked one-story with a slanted porch. They'd moved up to Colorado from a commune down in New Mexico. They talked a lot about digging cisterns, bulk rice, and Jesus, and they served the best broiled chicken and wild rice I've ever eaten. Before and after dinner, Ted jammed his fist into twelve-packs of Pabst Blue Ribbon producing one can after another. I spent many nights passed out on a consignment store couch in his living room.

Years later, I asked him to baptize me. His qualifications were that he himself had been baptized in a frozen river after breaking the ice with a sledgehammer. We did mine in a lake in New Mexico along a shore of preserved dinosaur tracks. There's a photo of me that day doing back flips off a rock with another Pabst drinker, a tall stalky kid with jet-black hair and a mandela of a smile named

Sam. Sam had driven me to the lake on the back of a 1972 Honda 250. Last I heard, he was in mime school in Paris. Later I found out I was the first person Ted had baptized. My mother also told me I'd already been baptized when I was a baby. Due to astronomically high blood pressure, Ted drank only decaf and non-alcoholic beer. It worked. He got down to 180/140. He gave me a cup of drip-filtered Folgers in a pastel cup with a long poem on the side. He got the cup in the divorce.

In the middle of a couch saddled with blankets, Jacob sat watching a rerun of *ESPN Baseball Tonight*. He was a slight kid with a mitt of black hair (like Sam, but shorter) and a wary, fur-born demeanor. His mouth and nose were narrow. With a set of long whiskers, he'd be cute. He had small, dark, beckoning eyes. He wore an Adidas visor, a T-shirt, and shorts. A light jacket lay on his lap.

I asked him. "How's the foot? Are you riding your bike?"

"I've been running."

"I thought you might give up running." He'd broken his ankle on a trail run in the spring. The guy he was running with was a former Pan-Am games medalist, former professional mountain runner in Europe, Masters world record holder and the U.S. Masters Mountain Running Champion who made a living trading stamps from a house he bought near the gator farm. He carried Jacob out of the mountains on his back. Jacob's Gator bio reads: "Jacob Nelson was raised in Illinois and came to the San Luis Valley to manage the fish farm after graduating college with a degree in fish biology. He has since studied at Adams State College to become a science teacher and just landed his first job at Sierra Grande High School in Ft. Garland. Jacob hopes to keep working at the farm during the summers especially to meet the different people who visit from all over the world." I'm not sure how Jake controlled a classroom of middle school thugs, except that the core of his being emanated pure intentions that must have somehow unmarrowed the sympathy of troubled youth.

"Have you guys had a lot of mice this year?" I asked.

"Not us. The ferrets catch them."

"Where are they?"

"Around, somewhere."

"Do you ever see them?"

"You see them now and then. Sometimes you don't see them, you just hear them—digging around. They love to get into stuff."

"So, are they kind of like cats?"

"Not really." He stared at the TV.

The last time I was at Ted and Jacob's, they were watching *ESPN Baseball Tonight*. I asked him, "Didn't you watch this last night?"

"Yeah."

"That's why I don't have TV. When I'm at a hotel, I just watch *Sports Center* over and over again."

"I do that everyday."

"If I had a TV, I'd never write anything."

"I like it as a source of information," Jacob said, his eyes glazed by the saccharin glow.

I went out to tell Vreni Ted wasn't ready. "Want to go to a yard sale?" I asked. We shuffled cattywampus across a dust-tracked intersection to an unfenced yard of fine dirt drifting against the skirts of a late model manufactured home. I took my poetry cup. A row of card tables was set up in front of boxes spilling unfolded clothes. We met Larry, a soft-faced man with a Texas deer-lease beard wearing striped, grey running sweats and a belly-stained T-shirt. His square tinted bifocals were topped by a mesh-backed "Great Sand Dunes" ball cap. He smoked a Swisher Sweet cigar that had been pulled from its plastic tip.

"Yeah, I worked at the gator farm for seven years," he mumbled.

Despite myself, I picked up a pocket watch.

"I collect eagles," he said. "The whole house is eagle stuff. I'm sort of upgrading now. Getting rid of the cheap stuff. I just ordered some plates from Courier and Ives. My kids gave me that watch for Christmas because there was an eagle on it. They were trying to be nice, you know."

I thumbed a deep scratch on the face and, despite myself, asked if it had a battery.

"You know, they stick a little piece of plastic in the pin to keep it from starting," Larry said. He shadowed my every move with seeming radar vision which told where my eyes paused. "That Osterizer is brand new. My wife just got a new one....My dog chewed the corner of that tool box, but it still works....My wife has Avon catalogs with a lot more stuff inside if your wife wants to order anything."

To be polite, Vreni asked if they had any Skin-so-Soft. Larry dug through a box of perfume bottles shaped like race cars and Eiffel towers. "We don't have any here, but we can order some."

I tried as hard as I could to avoid looking at two greasy electric chainsaws under a table. (Why are chainsaws irresistible?)

"I had more dresses with sequins," Larry mumbled, when Vreni got near a box. "I got 'em from a dead lady over in Saguache. They were all triple X. She sold them on the Internet to homosexuals in New York. I wish I had another ton of sequin dresses. She had all those Disney clothes in that box over there, too. Course, I already picked out the good ones."

I got on a stairstepper-like contraption, grabbing its vertical oars.

"You move those like you're skiing," Larry said. "I also have the complete Harley-Davidson 50th Anniversary Collection," he mumbled abstractly. "All twenty models."

I seriously considered the Joe Weider weight bench. "Look," I said to Vreni, "the butterfly attachments are actually still attached."

"You have a weight bench."

"Not with butterfly attachments."

"I can save it for you," Larry interjected.

"Too bad the car is full," Vreni said.

I hoped my cold decaf meant Ted was almost ready. As we were leaving, a little boy in dungarees and a striped shirt ran screaming from the back of the house, stopped in his tracks when he saw Larry, and screamed more. There was a dirt skid mark from the crown of his dark crew cut down across his cheek and his nose to the opposite side of his chin. Tears filled his large, gray eyes. It was hard to guess his age. I saw him run, but he seemed preverbal. "He's a tough kid." Larry said. The kid turned and walked away, apparently unbothered by the dirt on his face. Larry promised he'd be out every day for the rest of the summer if I wanted that watch. "And I have another coffee cup just like that one if you want a pair," he said.

Vreni told me it was the first garage sale she'd ever been to that she didn't buy anything. I felt bad, too, but I was thinking about one of those electric chainsaws.

As we loaded Ted and Jacob's stuff I realized I forgot firewood. I asked Ted if he had any firewood. He disappeared.

"Will we be able to have a fire?" Jacob asked.

"Is there a fire ban?" I asked.

"I don't know. Has there been a lot of rain this year?"

"Well, more than last year, but last year was the worst drought in fifty years."

"Does the county determine if there's a fire ban or do they decide that at the dunes."

"I'm not sure."

"What if the county doesn't have one and the dunes does. Can we have a fire anyway?"

"I think you can cook in the grills provided, or if you have your own gas grill or charcoal grill. Pat's bringing his."

"Are the rocks clean?"

"They looked okay to me," I shrugged.

"So there is a fire ban."

"I think so."

"Pat's bringing the grill. So, we won't need any firewood anyway. Where's Ted?"

"He went around back to get firewood."

I found him there. He was breaking dead branches over his knee and fitting broken boards into a milk crate. I told him we thought there was a fire ban. With terrific energy, he continued to break branches over his knee.

"Are you sure? There's been a lot of rain this year," he said.

"Yeah, but last year was the worst drought in fifty years."

"So does the county determine if there's a fire ban or do they decide that at the dunes?"

"We aren't sure."

"Well, if the county says there isn't and the dunes says there is, maybe we can have one anyway. Who's gonna know?"

"I think we can cook in the grills provided, or if we have our own grill."

"So, you think there's a fire ban."

"I think so, but Pat's bringing a grill so we won't need any firewood."

"Is it propane?"

"Yeah."

"Are the rocks clean?"

"I think they're okay."

"Well, let's take it anyway."

I didn't want to contribute to anyone's high blood pressure, so I loaded the milk crate of twigs and sticks in the back of the Buick.

You can see the dunes from almost anywhere in the valley, which means if the dunes were in Connecticut, you could see them from almost anywhere in the state. South of the sand, the sawed-up Sangres rose out of New Mexico. They were once towering domes twice their present height. Looking down from an airplane, the massifs look like frighteningly decayed molars with silvery lakes for fillings. After a granite upthrust, a wall of dark summits topping out at timberline extends northward to the dunes. Behind the sand formations there's a blunt gap, Mosca Pass. The mountains corner northwesterly at this low point, and another gunsight notch interrupts them again within a few miles. This is Medano Pass. Here the range corners again hard to the Northwest. Beyond the dunes, the range climbs to high grey thrones and tatty spines. In a land of prevailing northeasterly winds the sand stops at these mountains. It piles up seven hundred feet high like a beige blanket kicked into a corner. The sky over the mountains was as blue as a carpenter's chalk line.

All the windows were open and the plastic was flapping in the back and the radio was turned up, but there was lots of loud talking.

I said, "Did you know that the Great Sand Dunes were formed in one huge storm that lasted three to seven days and had winds over two hundred miles an hour?"

"Really?" Jacob asked me. "Where did you hear that?"

"I didn't," I said. "I just made it up. But I think it's possible. I read this book about super storms that could be triggered by global warming. They say that contrary to common sense, what might do us all in isn't that we'll all roast because it gets hotter and hotter. What will happen is that the warming will cause radical atmospheric disturbances at the poles that trigger a super cold storm that will blanket the Northern Hemisphere in thirty feet of snow. And if it doesn't melt right way—or if it melts part of the way and then freezes, into solid ice—it will reflect the sun that normally heats the ground and we'll be in the next ice age immediately. That's where I got the idea that maybe the dunes could have formed in one storm."

Ted said, "Did you hear the one about the two Eskimos who are freezing on a hunting trip and decide to start a fire in their kayak, which, of course, burns a hole in the kayak and the kayak sinks? The moral of the story is, 'You can't have your kayak and heat it, too.'" This leads to an elaborate joke about two identical twins—Juan and Amal—given up for adoption at birth. Later in life the biological mother is able to find her son Juan, but is unable to locate the other boy. Punch line: "Don't worry about it. If you've seen Juan, you've seen Amal."

"Did you know you could fit the whole state of Connecticut inside the valley?" I asked.

In unison everyone groaned, "Yes!"

"Did I already tell you that?" I asked.

In unison everyone groaned, "Yes!"

The road to the dunes was yet another gunbarrel in a valley of gunbarrels: miles of pewter gravel mashed into a skin of tar through hundreds of square miles of unattractive dirt, which got flakier, more alkaline, and more unattractive the farther east we went. The bar ditch was sprinkled with locoweed. Tiny pinkish paddles spoked out from sprite clusters of vivid purple. We passed the entrance to San Luis Lakes, a sump of percolated ground water, a mini-Mono. I remembered a story of a kid drowning there. Right off the boat ramp. The father said he turned around for a second. When a kid drowns someone always says they just turned around for a second. That's exactly what I mean. Things that we think take a long time actually happen really fast. Like ice ages and sand dunes. By the time we realize it, it's done. The lake was practically dried up by drought. That helped kill all the suckers. Fishermen were excited about the possibility of the lake refilling. They wanted to restock it with trout. That poor father.

The road hopped a cattle guard. A narrow canal brimming with blue water crawled straight south across high desert that got less than seven inches of rain per year. Wells at the north end of the valley pumped into the canal and the water supplemented the Rio Grande, thirty miles away. The canal was designed to save water, which, in theory, would otherwise get sucked up by salt grasses and greasewood roots and get wasted to transvaporation.

The mountains looked like real mountains as we got closer— bare arêtes, transverse crotches, steep draws, harrowed chutes, pommeled cliffs. Anything facing south was exposed stone. On north sides, conifer draped deep pleats that drop thousands of feet out to open flats. Behind the cleavage of Ellington and California Peak, we saw the desiccated and splintered iliac of Mt. Lindsey (14,042). I thought about that Paul Simon song and I wondered why Cristo got misspelled in the lyrics. Though we were still miles away, the contours, textures, and height of the dunes impressed. The tallest, nested in the interior of thirty square miles of high sand dunes, is shaped like a star. Approaching midday, the sand was a little dull, not the yellow or gold you might expect. Black-eyed sunflowers appeared in the bar ditches. The road split sandy hillocks of bleached grasses and straggled shrubs. We were onto the "Sand Sheet," sand that surrounds the main dunes like the train of a wedding dress. The Sheet comprises over half of the total sand deposit of the Great Sand Dunes. Including the Sheet, sand covers sixty square miles. We jumped another cattleguard, into buffalo country, the Medano and Zapata ranches. Fifty thousand acres each, both were new additions (via the Nature Conservancy) to the Park and Preserve. About twenty years ago, historic Zapata Ranch was developed as a sort of country club. A golf course was built with a tony inn, restaurant, and spa. (You can still find brochures in the Hooper post office.) The club attracted Japanese investors in the '80s who foreclosed by the early '90s, which is when someone brought in buffaloes. They still wandered the ranch's open range, including the decommissioned golf course.

"Hey, Ted, remember when I hit the buffalo?"

"I remember that," Ted said. "The next morning it was so cold your emergency brake froze and there was so much snow on the street the car would only drive in circles." He laughed, just as he had that morning. From almost exactly the same spot where the buffalo almost killed me, a poet visualized what it must have been like to see buffalo grazing in the valley one hundred and fifty years ago. Inspired by the domestic herd, she wrote:

> Twenty or thirty of them north on the roadway
> looking like statues that move
> and stir dust clouds and rises.
> I step from the car
> find them in my lense
> move closer.
>
> Their dust settles over me
> clouds my glasses, covers
> A hundred years and more
> And despite Nikon and Nikes
> I am there.

The poem ends with a beautiful line from a pioneer mother's dreams: *the moon paints buffalo shadows on a cabin wall.* The poem could go back ten thousand years, to the end of the last ice age, and a Folsom woman dreaming buffalo shadows. Points and fire pits turn up all around the dunes. The landscape was lush back then. The dunes themselves are reported to have formed about twelve thousand years ago, but what if...? What if Folsom came thirteen thousand years ago? Then, that Folsom woman saw it happening. She was there.

At a T we headed north and passed the "Oasis Motel," a double-wide in the middle of nowhere remodeled into two sunny rooms with log siding. I break into falsetto.

Midnight at the oasis
Send your camel to bed
Shadows painted our faces
Traces of romance in our heads

Everyone laughed, so I sang again.

Midnight at the oasis
Send your camel to bed
Shadows painted our faces
Traces of romance in our heads

I knew if I kept doing it, they would quit laughing by the fourth time. Around the seventh or ninth time, they would laugh again. This is the well known Torture Theory of Humor.

Midnight at the oasis
Send your camel to bed
Shadows painted our faces
Traces of romance in our heads

Two miles up the road, we passed the Oasis RV Park/Camp-ground & General Store. Large signs announced GIFTS, SHOWERS, TEE-PEES, GROCERIES, HOMEMADE PIES, LODGING, GASOLINE (a pump of Unleaded and a pump of Midgrade—"Pre-pay," "Please do not leave pump unattended"). A post and beam porch fronted a stockade of milled logs and a Propanel roof. There were signs everywhere: DINING ROOM, ICE CREAM, GIFTS, TOURS, CURIOS, FIREWOOD, CAMPING, ICE. Sand and cigarette butts almost bur-ied the parking chocks out front. Apparently butts have the exact aerodynamic properties of sand. If Folsom man were a smoker, the dunes might be constructed of Marlboro filters. An "out of order" pay phone dangled by the front door. The hose of a coin-operated air compressor hung at the far end of the porch. At the near end, two plastic deck tables matched plastic molded chairs. A small neon Miller sign glowed in one window. Budweiser glowed three windows down. A "message center" with two rusty clips screwed to peg board and a small chalk board looked to have been long out of use. A pastel rendering of the dunes had been erased. Beside it was tacked a faded *RV America Guide Map to the United States*.

We didn't go in. I'd been in there. I knew what we'd find: silver plated collectable spoons, thimbles, sheriff badges, stained glass Nite Lites, mesh baseball caps, suction "Indian Archery" sets, portable Electronic Solitaire, Fling Toss, Slinkies, magnetic chess, Tee-Pee Tots (bean bag dolls with rubber skin the color of Ovaltine), beaded necklaces, ammo for your cap gun, ceramic accent candles (Southwest themes), carved ironwood figurines (moose, bear, owl, bighorn, elk), T-shirts, wolf and Navajo patterned rugs, books, (*Roadside Geology, Indian Doctor, Log Cabin Pioneers: Stories, Songs, and Sayings, Buffalo Soldiers, The Rocky Mountain Berry Book*, and *Lonesome Dove*), nature posters, bookmarkers, postcard packets (same subjects as the ironwood carving plus bobcat, cougar, bison, eagle, raccoon), panorama postcards, bronze western plaques, dream catchers, hypo-allergenic "Colorado" ear rings, turquoise rings, shapeable straw hats ("Go ahead and bend it, roll it any way you want it"), pine tree seeds, hippie purses, sundry camping gear, wind chimes (stained glass, wire work, porcelain, and wooden), travel sewing kits, RV shaped salt and pepper shakers (Airstreams, I think), piggy banks, gag shot glasses, gas cans, corkscrews, RV/Marine toilet paper, kites, toe mood rings, one leather bull whip, the usual truck stop snacks and drinks (Red Hot cheese puffs, jerky, gummy worms, chocolate milk, etc.). Note: The Oasis does not take local checks.

Before we entered the park, the habitat shifted to piñon and juniper hillsides. The dunes are so massive they blocked views of the northern end of the valley. Except for niches of green, the sand was completely bare, miles of pastel, surprisingly rosy sidewalls and pitches varying subtly from taupe to cashmere, the kind of colors you'd expect to find in a chalk drawing of sand dunes. But every drawing or painting I have seen of the dunes is bad, a caricature. There is no palette with the nuance of the sand. Paint isn't agile enough for it. The sand's force and grace might be better portrayed in dance, ballet. Photography of the dunes from any angle or distance (and in any season) is striking, but is also small tribute. The lost scale neutralizes the image and reduces the image maker to unwitting satirist. The colossal sand peaks are for the naked eye. They dwarf art. A single dune looks like a wave at its apogee, but dune after dune fused together are nothing like an ocean. They looked settled, not swollen. It was obvious they were formed by constant, fluid turbulence—algorithmic, like water—but the sand does things an ocean could never do. They mimic, but they surpass a sea.

A kind-faced squatty woman in a straight brimmed Ranger cap greeted us at the gate. She wore makeup.

"How are the ski conditions?" I asked.

Her face went blank. She searched below her counter as if there was an information sheet she'd misplaced. Finally she said, "I saw someone with a surfboard."

The Roadmaster slid by the Visitor Center, remodeled after a fire scorched a corner of the Park a couple of years back. The architecture, paneled stucco, might be described as a blend of Santa Fe Square and Hollywood "Stargate," or Future Shock/ Egyptian, or Post-Deco-Pueblo-Office-Park. Not long after the fire, the Park was quarantined because two employees developed bizarre lesions that ate through their skin and muscle. One died. Leprosy was 'officially' discounted. The story faded. The gates reopened. The center's movie theatre still shows an interpretive film produced in the '60s narrated by my old college opera coach. In four lessons he urged me to roll my hips forward and sing Italian arias through my "mask" while he punched me gently in the diaphragm. I seldom succeeded, but he once scolded a resonance from me so powerful I almost fell over dizzy, my head buzzing like a hive of bees. He was quite perturbed when I laughed and couldn't continue.

The piñon and juniper mixed with modest aspen stands as we turned left toward the base of the dunes and the "Picinic Loop," where narrow-leafed cottonwoods and willows grew between bunkers of sand sprinkled with rice grass and scurf pea. Less than fifty yards from the tables, famous seasonal Medano Creek (the creek with waves!), wide and shallow, spilled across its flat sand bed. Beyond, the landscape was pure sand—endless, climbing sand. The station wagon barely fit the narrow chip-seal of the loop.

I was looking for Pat. "Are we getting a tree spot or a ramada?" I asked someone, anyone.

"Is that what they're called?" Vreni asked.

"Yeah. I didn't know that. I just remembered it from Colossal Cave. They call their visitor center a ramada. Pat was going to save us a spot, but I don't see him."

"He's following you," Vreni said.

Ted said, "He's probably wondering why you keep driving around and around this loop."

Jacob said, "He might be wondering why you're going the wrong way."

I noticed the faded arrows painted on the chip seal were pointing at me. "What arrows?" I said. I nudged into a sandy pull out. Pat came up with his window down.

"Do we want trees or a ramada?" he asked.

I was impressed. "How did you know they were called that?"

Pat said, "Did you know you're going the wrong way?"

Finally, we backed up to a nice double ramada—six picnic tables, three to each ramada—close to bathrooms and a short hike to the dunes. Jacob said, "The Buick needs one of those beacons, like a bulldozer, to let people know that this thing is backing up."

There was chattering and gaggling, and everyone took a turn goo-goo-gahing with Katherine as she toddled around the coolers and bags of food. We set up under one ramada. Ted got into the non-alcoholic beer right away. Since Jacob wasn't climbing, I offered him a Negra. "Do you think this will keep the rain out?" I asked Pat, looking at the ramada's cover.

"Some," he said.

Page said, "Isn't ramada a nautical term?"

"I thought it was a country in Africa," Ted said.

"No, it's a hotel chain," Jacob said.

Ted said, "Isn't it the ninth month of the Mohammedan year? You're supposed to fast from sunrise to sunset. It means 'the hot month.'"

"That's armada," Pat corrected Page. She laughed.

"Don't feel bad," I said. "I didn't know what they were called until we visited Colossal Cave."

"I don't feel bad," she said. "Oh! Cheese Puffs!"

"You like cheese puffs?" I said.

"I love them."

"I can eat an entire bag, and I do—once a year."

"And these are the perfect cheese puffs, the cheap bloaty ones."

"Real cheese puffs," I nodded. "PUFEE CHEEZ brand, 'Super Pack.'"

"So what is a ramada?" Vreni asked.

Ted said, "It's from the Spanish ramo or rama. One's masculine. One's feminine. In English, it's ramose, which means 'having many branches.' The Latin root is the same for all three: ramus, which just means 'branch'."

"So, if you're named Ramon, is that from the same root?"

"Ramon might be a branch of the root word. Get it? Branch.

Root." Ted grinned jutting his chin my way. It's the same grin he had when I was driving in circles in the snow in front of his house the morning after I was almost killed by the buffalo.

"I get it. Family tree/etymology pun."

"A left handed Leo pun," he smiled.

"So that's where ramify and ramiform and ramification and ramulose probably come from," Jacob added. "They all mean 'to divide into branches' or 'to develop extensions.' Ramus is actually a term used in Biology."

"Do you think they have ramadas in Spain?" I asked. "Or did the Spanish build them over here because there was no shade in Arizona?"

"Or did they get the idea from the Pueblos?"

"How did bighorn sheep get to be called rams?" Page asked. "What does a male sheep have to do with a branch?"

"Well," Ted said, "men have their very own branch." He was grinning again.

Vreni said. "That's gross, Ted,"

I said, "Well, in the crusades they used tree trunks—that is, giant branches—to crash through castle gates during a siege. So the word for branch then became a verb related to an action the noun had taken on: ramming. Then when the Spanish first saw bighorns and saw them crashing into each other with their horns—just like a tree trunk into a castle gate—they transmogrified the verb back into a noun and called the males the rams. It was probably even more meaningful that horns are like branches growing out of a bighorn's head, so—as the Spanish saw it—the sheep were using the branches on their heads to crash into each other. Thus, the verb was transmogrified back into the noun for male sheep."

"Transmogrified, huh?" Page said, laughing. "I definitely don't believe that,"

"Hey," I said. "It's my party and I'll bullshit if I want to."

"So, why do they call them rams in Ireland?" Ted said.

"Oh, that's from the Greek raam," Jacob said.

"What does it mean in Greek?" Page asked.

"I think it just means 'Male sheep,'" Jacob said.

"It's from the zodiac," Ted said, as though we had all missed the obvious. "Aries is the ram. It's been around since domestication."

"Where did they get the branches?" I asked Pat. "You see these things in the middle of the reservation. There isn't a tree for a hundred miles."

"You could use short branches off of shrubs. That's why the designs are ribbed in two or three parts."

"I wonder why they turned the branches diagonally."

"Some are straight," Pat says, "It's stronger diagonally. It stabilizes the roof and keeps it from twisting in the wind."

"That seems like overkill."

"Not if a dust devil comes along."

"Wouldn't that just pick it up off the ground?" Page asked.

"That's why the Pueblo invented rebar and reinforced concrete." I said. "Did you know that the timbers used for the first church at Acoma were harvested in Colorado over near Chimney Rock?"

"Right," Page said. "I'm not falling for that."

"Actually, that's true" Pat said. "The Acoma part, not the rebar part."

I had to ask Ted, "What's the difference between a masculine and a feminine branch?"

"One hits you over the head; the other hits you between the legs," Ted quipped.

"That's gross, Ted," Vreni said.

I sang:

> *Midnight at the oasis*
> *Send your camel to bed*
> *Shadows painted our faces*
> *Traces of romance in our heads*

I leaned my Fatboys bottoms up against the tail gate of the Buick. I scraped the bases thoroughly with a plastic scrapper (to get spring wax off). Next, I scoured the bases with a Scotchbrite pad. Finally, I wrapped 150-grit Aluminum Oxide sand paper around the scrapper and made three passes over the bases, pressing firmly. (I'd have done a finish buff if I'd had some Swix Fiberlene.) The ski bases were dry as plywood. I asked Vreni where the camcorder was. It was in the car. I handed it to her.

"Document, please," I said.

"Document what?" she said. "People are eating, and you're goofing around with your skis."

"Document. If it's not documented, it never happened."

I gave Jacob a two-way radio. "You're 'Base Camp.' Pat and I are 'Expedition'," I told him. "Whatever you do, don't let Ted handle the radio."

"Cool," he giggled. "Why can't Ted use it?"

"Never let Ted get near technology," I said. "Let's try a test run: 'Expedition to Base camp.'"

"This is Base Camp," Jacob giggled.

"Base Camp, can we get a weather report?"

"Incoming, Expedition. The window has closed. Abort! Abort!"

"Good."

Medano Pass Road winds between the dunes and the mountains. It's four-wheeling in sand. The Park Service recommends that tires be flattened to 20 PSI to avoid getting stuck. A "Point of No Return" sign is posted where the road gets narrow and the sand ruts get deep. Pat was a little nervous about messing up his new truck, especially when the curves and whoop-dee-doos became exceptionally soft. I got out and ran ahead at a blind corner to test the sand with my feet and waved him on. I'd been told sand skiing was a slow-motion affair and only the steepest wall would do. It needed to be tall, too, we agreed, tall enough to make the hike worthwhile.

We passed several enormous canted dunes, their faces dished like woks. Not steep enough. The road narrowed between cottonwoods. I urged Pat to keep going. I remembered a massive wall rising straight up from the base of Medano Creek. I wondered if it was still there. It was. Pat backed into a pullout. Jacob scrambled out the back of the truck. Ted stood on the tailgate, a Sharps dangling in his hand. Page unloaded Katherine and headed for the creek. Pat danced around swiping bugs from his bare legs.

"The way to set the record is to traverse it," I said looking up. "That way you won't splat at the bottom."

"What record?" he said.

"The World Sand Speed Skiing Record."

"Yeah," Ted said. "Ride it like a pipeline."

"I didn't bring my GPS," Pat said. "I could have measured your speed."

Ted said, "You can do that?"

I turned to Jacob. "See what I mean? No technology near him."

The dune was sun washed, between three hundred and four hundred feet high. Not much compared to a ski slope, but it was steep. It was already scribbled with two sets of awkward looking ski tracks. They looked unsatisfying. I didn't pack much: boots, skis, and a 34 oz. Nalgene bottle of diluted Gatorade. I forgot a strap to tie my ski tips together, so I laid the skis flat on the pack and clipped the compression straps under the toe bindings. Side by side they were almost as wide as a snowboard.

"Documentation," I reminded Vreni. She filmed. "Twenty years from now people will laugh at our clothes and our equipment and our car and how skinny we are. By then it might be illegal to ski on the dunes and we'll be considered really despicable and stupid people for upsetting the entire eco-balance of the planet by violating the natural creep of the sand. The demise of the biosphere will come back to July 29, 2005. The Butterfly Effect: the stirring of a grain of sand in Colorado sets off a hurricane in the Atlantic. Our grandchildren will gawk at the thought of our thoughtlessness, but that won't matter because we were skinny once, and we had all our teeth, and they'll be amazed. They'll ask their mommies and daddies why people were so dumb back then, and mommy will say, 'That weren't bad people. Everyone was dumb back then.' And the grandchildren will say, 'Everyone skied on the sand dunes?' 'Well, not everyone,' mommy will say. 'Just your granddaddy and a few other nuts.' For the record: I want everyone watching twenty years from now to know that the tsunami already happened. That was not our fault. And while we are at it, I just want everyone to remember this song:

> Midnight at the oasis
> Send your camel to bed
> Shadows painted our faces
> Traces of romance in our heads

'Does nuts mean granddaddy was crazy, mommy?' 'Go to sleep, honey.' 'Mommy, if granddaddy was crazy, does that mean we'll all be crazy someday?' 'Go to sleep, honey.'"

Vreni asked how long the hike would take. She was worried she might miss us and have to listen to another speech about documentation. Pat asked if I were taking extra clothing. I wasn't sure what he meant. It was two in the afternoon. I was wearing tennis shoes, green safari shorts, an old yellow polo shirt, and a wide brimmed hat with the top cut out of it. "You mean like a parka?" I teased him.

Vreni said, "What are you going to do to keep from getting road rash when you...never mind." I was affronted that my own wife hinted I might fall.

I said, "I plan to fall on my chest."

On the short trail to the creek, we passed a sign that read, "Hot

Sand/Lightning." They say the sand can get up to 140 degrees. Another sign read "Extremely Soft Sand Ahead," which set me to wondering about hard sand. The creek was ankle deep and perfectly clear. At the far edge, I stepped up onto a dry cut bank. Pat was behind me, kissing Page goodbye. They stood in the middle of the warm flowing water. Katherine sat in the creek next to them with her lips in the water, gurgling and drinking as tiny waves passed.

The morning's skiers had been Telemarkers; they climbed with their skies on. As I climbed, I tried to find a packed layer under their old tracks. The tracks traversed for about two hundred yards up onto a high ridge. My feet sank. My shoes were soon filled and heavy. I wasn't wearing socks. I knew Pat wasn't either. He wore some rubber sandals. I called back to warn him. He waved. "I have socks," he said, and unshouldered his pack.

Every step smeared. It was like climbing a stairway of loose oats with sad irons for slippers. Soon, my shoes were filled and heavy. To make any progress, I had to kick with the outside edge of my uphill foot (my right) and with the inside edge of my downhill foot. There was nothing to do but hunch and aim for blue sky. I huffed on, using my poles like a cross country skier. The fat skis towered over me. My pack felt like it was stuffed with bowling balls. All I saw was the next step. I stopped once to see how far back Pat was. He followed my tracks in his wool knee socks.

Up on the ridge, I was out of sight of everyone below. Wide effluvial sheets of sand undulated above and below me. The wind whispered on the sand. I felt an aphasic swaying sensation. That might have been the wind catching the skis. The sky was as blue as painter's tape. The ski tracks etched pale switchbacks toward a high, white sun. I'd given up on the tracks being firmer footing, but they did appear to mark the easiest route up. I climbed again. My heart dribbled like a basketball against the back of my sternum. Rushing blood swooshed in my ears. My breathing became whistley and hot.

Head down, I noticed the sand was not pure. The buff color that dominates from a distance is traced with black material throughout. It looks like graphite dumped from a pencil sharpener.[26] Whatever it was, it intersticed the ruffled surface like the grey striations in a trout fillet, and acted exactly like sand.

I planted a pole beside something that looked like a cat turd. I picked it up. It was a fulgurite, petrified lightning. Fulgurites form when lightning strikes sand. The sand is superheated (lightning is five times hotter than the sun), melts and fuses. A delicate, hacky, rough, tubular nugget is left behind. Sand remnants adhere to the outside, but the interior of the tube is smooth and glassy, as if glazed and kiln-fired. Fulgurites have been found as branch-like pipes as big as and as long as a human forearm. The world record, composed of two branches of sixteen and seventeen feet, was found near Blanding Camp Florida in 1997. They haven't found a museum with enough space to display it. Some fulgurites survive as fossils, up to 250 million years old. Colors vary from black to grey to clear. The one I found was about an inch-and-a-half long. The tube was open on one end (some are open at both ends). It looked like wet Frosted Flakes had been squeezed tightly in someone's fingers and then burned from the inside out by a small explosion. People buy and sell fulgurites on the Internet, for five to six dollars a gram. (For some reason the ones open at both ends fetch a higher price.) I pictured fulgurite dealers standing around on beaches during lightning storms, scrambling over each other the way kayakers fight for baseballs Barry Bonds hit into the San Francisco harbor. I'd seen fulgurites at the Visitor's Center, but I never knew anyone who found one. Since it was right on the surface, the one I found must have been formed recently. I felt lucky to find it before the blowing sand covered it. I put it in a side pocket of my shorts and reminded myself to give it to Vreni when I got to the bottom. I

26 It's magnetite.

looked up. The sky was still as blue as painter's tape.

At the top, I dropped my pack, unloaded the skis and boots, and gulped Gatorade. I saw dunes upon dunes upon dunes. From the high vantage, they did look, as Zebulon Pike described them in 1807, "like a sea in a storm." (He was trespassing in Spanish territory.) To a skier, they also looked like a sea of snowdrifts.

"I knew it would be hot," Pat said. "You know the sand can get up to one-forty."

"How hot do you think it is right now?"

"One thirty-nine."

I heard electronic squawking. I asked if Pat had the radio. He handed it to me.

"Base Camp, this is Expedition," I said.

Jacob answered. "Expedition, this is Base Camp."

"Base Camp, could you send a couple of snow cones up here?"

"Expedition, beware of heat stroke. If heat stroke threatens you must abort."

"10-4, Base Camp." I handed the radio back to Pat, but I still heard squawking. "Do you hear that?" I asked him. We looked around. "There," he said, pointing. Down on the four-wheel-drive road, an open roofed tour bus with about twenty-five passengers was headed for the creek. The squawk was the voice of the driver/guide on a megaphone.

"I don't believe it," I said.

"Looks like we're going to have an audience," Pat said.

We took a couple of snap shots of each other with Pat's digital camera and booted up. I told him about the coyote I saw up on the dunes years ago.

"I doubt one coyote would hurt you," he said.

"I wondered what might have happened if it hadn't been alone."

"Probably nothing. If they attack something big, it's usually because it's weak or injured."

I didn't tell him that I'd been running naked and my soul was wounded and any coyote with half a spirit would have known it on sight. I asked Pat, "Do you think a coyote could tell the difference between a human with clothes on and a human with clothes off?"

Pat laughed. "I don't know. Why do you ask?"

"No reason. Did you know the Jicarrila Apache used sand from these dunes for ceremonial purposes? They still do."

"I did read that in the brochure they gave us at the gate," he said. "How many turns do you think we'll get?"

"I have no idea," I said.

"You've done this before, right."

"I've never done this."

"I thought you'd done this before."

"Nope. Always wanted to."

Pat was quiet for a second, regrouping his thoughts. "I wonder how many people have done it," he asked.

"More than you think," I said. "I've seen a picture from the early 1930s of three guys standing way up on the sand with their skis on. Are you having as hard a time with this as I am?" I was prying the shell of a boot apart and trying to get my sweaty bare foot in.

"The sand doesn't help," Pat said. "I might wear some knee-high hose next time."

I didn't say anything, but I decided it was actually a good idea. Finally buckled up and snapped into my bindings, I stood on my skis on the sand. I tried to slide them back and forth. Nothing. They stuck like scrambled eggs to a camp pan. I looked at Pat. "If this really sucks, we're only doing it once." I pointed the skis straight down hill. "Dune skiing is just like alligator wrestling, Pat. You have to know what you want, don't hesitate and don't let go, for he who hesitates gets bit. Once you jump, stay committed. Most people are physically capable of dune skiing. Overcoming their mental fears is the hard part."

I pushed hard with my poles, scooting myself onto the steep pitch. The skis began to flow. I discovered skis on sand do not skim the surface. They don't slide. When the slope gets steep enough, the layer of sand sticking to the base of the skis releases from the layer underneath. Then more layers underneath start to flow. Basically, you ride on top of a stubborn, slow motion wave. It's tectonic.

The tips of the skis wanted to dig in, so I jockeyed my weight onto my heels. This helped a little, but it made turning difficult. When I changed direction at all, the skis threatened to stop dead and throw me. I was not getting it. I tried keeping my feet closer together, balancing my weight equally on both and leaning back a little bit—a technique that wasn't enjoyable but sometimes works when snow is unskiably thick. I estimated I was traveling about eight or nine miles an hour.

About half way down I hit a large patch of scattered grass. The sand in the grass was firm and felt slicker. I picked up speed and I was able to lean forward. Scurfing out of the grass onto a steeper headwall, I tried working one ski at a time—an Old School racing technique. It resulted in a little more speed. It almost felt like skiing. By the end, I was linking turns. Top speed: fifteen miles per hour, maybe. I stopped at the creek edge and turned to see Pat making a couple of tripod-like stem turns. His pole baskets drug like the discs of a cultivator.

There was hooting, hollering, whistling, and clapping from the tour bus. "Bravo," someone shouted. An elderly man in a straw hat and large square sunglasses said, "Well, I can go back to Kansas and say I've seen something I've never seen before."

Pat and I sat by the creek, pried our boots off, wiped the sand off our skis and packed for another climb. Vreni stood in the creek with the camcorder, filming.

Ted and Jacob wandered out. Ted had his checkered shirt

wrapped around his head like an Arab. He said, "It sounded mighty lugubrious, if you asked me."

"What does that mean?" Vreni asked.

"Kind of sluggish," he said.

The climb had taken fifteen minutes, Vreni told us. It seemed longer. The second time, there was more wind. The blowing sand smelled like dried fish scales. Every sinking step seemed like a step deeper into oblivion. The Great Sand Dunes are one massive, aloof monument to inconsequentiality. When you walk out on dunes, you walk onto time—pure time, devoid of human activity. That's why I've always liked them. A little hike on the dunes reminds me that the whole human drama, from beginning to end, isn't such a big deal. It isn't the biggest deal in the universe, anyway.

As a whole, the formation is what geologists call a *draa*. A *draa* is a large sand dune many miles long and hundreds of feet deep. The word is most likely Arabic and may be related to the Old French word for drape which became, in English, drab. Drab means "grayish to yellowish brown" or "light olive brown or khaki color." In other words, the colors that occur in the mottle of sand. I could see how dunes might look like drapes billowing in the wind. Drab also means "dreary" in personality.

On the second run, Pat went first. I documented from the top using the video function of his digital camera. I skied straighter, purposely aiming for big patches of grass, and exaggerating the one-footed technique. It worked. I counted thirty-one turns. At the bottom, I reached into my side pocket to return Pat's camera. It was covered with glassy, sandy crumbs. My fulgurite. By the third run we made turns that looked like real skiing. The sand *whirrrped* under the skis. Every turn was a fart. I strung together thirty-eight farts while I sang:

> *Midnight at the oasis*
> *Send your camel to bed*

Shadows painted our faces
Traces of romance in our heads

By the end of our fourth run, we were getting the hang of it and it almost felt like skiing.

Back at the ramada, Pat grilled organic German-style sausages. Every bag of chips was opened. We drank the Sprite and the Coca-Cola from glass bottles, and debated. Half thought that recycled bottles are melted down and recast; the other half believed they were collected and washed. That's why the bases were scratched and worn out. The cost of a can of Coke was the aluminum, someone said. Did you know that some people think the reason that we won WWII was because the U.S. had built so many dams during the depression that by the time the war came we had a superior ability to produce electricity, which allowed us to manufacture aluminum aircraft at a dizzying rate. Some think the Grand Coulee alone won the war. Does recycling really take less energy—if you take into account the collection and transportation of millions of cans per day, maybe billions of cans per year? Why does Mexico still use bottles? I sat in a folding camp chair with the last Negra Modelo and the PUFEE CHEEZ Super Pack in my lap. The alcohol seeped into the walls of my dehydrated, sand-blasted heart like honey into Wonder Bread. My metaphysical central heating hummed as I imagined my orange smile. Ted and I blew out the candles on a black bottom and chocolate chip cheese cake.

"Doesn't this cheese cake have corn syrup in it?" Page teased.

"I hope so," I said. Ted and I ate the last two pieces. "Corn syrup! It's the equivalent of lead pipes in Rome."

I got the cordless drill and a pair of old wooden Nash children's water skis from the back of the Buick. I removed the rubber heels and the plastic tail fins. No one was really paying attention until I said, "Everybody ready?"

"For what?"

"For the first annual World Sand Speed Skiing Championships."

"I thought we just did that," Ted said.

"We were turning," I said. "To the dunes!"

"He's kidding, right?" Page said to Vreni.

"It's his party," she shrugged.

My friends, stuffed with sausage, chips, and cheesecake, moved like senior citizens snowshoeing across a Las Vegas ash tray. At the creek, we slipped off our shoes and rolled our trousers. The water was shoal shallow, as clear as a cornea and warm as old bath water.

"This water is clear as a cornea," I said.

"Clear as cornea syrup," Ted said.

"Funny," I said.

"Don't encourage him," Vreni said.

Ted said, "Do you know the difference between a corny joke and a cornea joke?"

I said, "Everyone can see what you mean?"

Ted said, "Did I tell you the one about the two Eskimos? The one that ends, 'You can't have your kayak and heat it too?'"

"Yes," everyone groaned.

"How about the one about the lost twin brothers Juan and Amal?"

"YES!" everyone groaned.

I asked if Vreni remembered the camcorder. She had.

The *draa* was half shadowed. It was the golden hour. The hour that you think about life and death at the same time. Another day was over but not quite yet. Scatterings of people, tiny looking, came down off the high dunes. They followed smeared lanes of tracks that snaked from the crests. You could hear the muffled farting under their feet and their garrulous laughing. The sand was cool, cooler in shady spots. The wind died to a breeze.

We found a drift of sand steep enough to slide on. Ted dragged an abandoned plastic sled someone left. He went first. The sand plowed up. He rocked back and forth. The sled inched down. He stretched his arms over his head like a teenager on a roller coaster. I set the water skis in his track. The rubber bindings fit like tight, cold slippers. I shuffled forward. They slid slower than an escalator. I tucked, sure I was the first person to water ski the sand dunes. Vreni filmed. I finished a second run with a flourish, popping up like a ski jumper. Ted went again. We estimated he hit four miles per hour.

I grabbed the tails of the water skis as Pat wriggled his feet in. I coached him, "It's all about the finish. Extend the arms. Poke your head to the sky and step out." He was fast, almost five miles per hour. The dismount was perfect. Page shuffled the skis forward before I could give her a boost and she slid in a sitting stance. She swiped her hair back and turned to wave to Katherine, who sat screaming in Pat's lap. Page pumped her arms. "Parallel! Parallel!" I urged her. "No snowplowing!" She finished with wide arms, turned and bowed and waved. We clapped wildly. Katherine wailed.

Bystanders wandered over. A pale, skinny, gray-headed man in white shorts, a blue polo shirt, and square photo-grey glasses begged to try. He showed his wife how to operate their digital camera. He crouched. His right foot balked. The skis side-slipped. At the bottom, he couldn't get out of the skis and he duck walked around until they shook off. The crowd cheered. First man over sixty to water ski the dunes.

Vreni didn't tuck. She wagged her arms and made shake-your-booty go-go moves. I teased her, "Disqualified!" I cajoled Jacob. He was tentative. "Turn your visor backwards for aerodynamics," I said. His skinny feet fit in the bindings as if they were flip flops. "Masai warriors who watch *Sports Center* do this," I told him. He bent as if he were picking up a quarter. Before I could back away, he farted—a little puffy, Negra Modelo, ferret fart. Everyone erupted, laughing. "He farted!" He staged a wipe out at the bottom, rolling, sand flying. I had to tell him he's disqualified. Not for farting—he didn't finish with at least one ski on.

The sun dipped lower, a large, silver zia resting on a high cusp of the *draa*. Our shadows were eighty yards long and thin as straws.

It was a quiet ride to the house. I had the radio turned low. Every five seconds, a mouse—some small as bugs, others as big as hamsters—dashed across the high beams.

I said, "When I went to buy mousetraps a woman in the store said she and her husband moved their haystack this spring and thousands of mice came out. She said cats showed up she'd never seen before and stuffed themselves for hours."

Vreni had dozed off.

I listened to KRDR—"*Top hits! Top of the Charts! Top of the Circle!*"—which was mixing Spanish techno with big band, classic rock, and folk. I liked the station because every now and then they played "Ben," the Academy Award-winning theme song from the movie featuring killer rats. (It was the sequel to *Willard*.) They also played the Bay City Rollers, the only rock group in kilts to ever have a top-ten hit. (*S-A-T-U-R-D-A-Y NIGHT!*) They played Tina Turner's cover of Robert Palmer's "Simply Irresistible." They sometimes played "Rocky Mountain High," but I hoped they wouldn't because I can't help singing along and I didn't want Vreni to wake up and find me crying.

I woke her up, anyway. I needed the conversation to keep myself awake. "Do you think we should invest in collectible plates?"

"No," she mumbled.

"Larry had collectible Harley-Davidson plates."

"Larry?"

"The guy at the yard sale."

"His name was Larry?"

"Yeah, Larry."

"You can get Harley-Davidson Plates?"

"Maybe it was eagles."

"You never smoked Swisher Sweets, did you?" she asked.

"At bachelor parties. I leave the plastic tips on, though. You know, Ted and Jacob don't have any mice."

"We're not getting ferrets," she said.

"Jacob says you hardly ever see them."

"No ferrets."

The radio reception took on static as we crested dark hills. More mice darted onto the chip-seal, confused by the headlights. Somehow the Roadmaster missed them all.

"That was a great day," I said.

Vreni reached across the bench seat and put her hand on my knee. "Happy birthday," she said.

"Isn't it weird that Ted and I have the same birthday fifteen years apart?"

"It's even weirder that he baptized you," she said.

"You know, I didn't know I was the first person he'd ever baptized," I said. "I thought he did it all the time. But that's okay. Did you know the Jicarilla Apache used and still use the sand from the Great Sand Dunes for ceremonial purposes?"

"I read that in the brochure."

"I wish they had said what for," I said.

Vreni nodded, or maybe she was just nodding off.

"Remember the time on the dunes?"

"Yes," she said.

"That was awesome."

"Yes, it was."

"Remember the time at the falls?"

"Yes," she said.

"Remember the time on the steps of the Lincoln Memorial?"

"Shut up," she said.

"Maybe we should have waited until it was dark."

"Shut up." She slept.

The static on the radio got stronger, punctuated by sharp squelches. I fine tuned the dial, and I thought I heard…then I was sure I heard it.

I heard

Midnight at the oasis…